Decisions
Getting What You Want

Decisions
Getting What You Want
Bruce Becker

YES DEAR

GROSSET & DUNLAP
A FILMWAYS COMPANY
Publishers • New York

For those

who have loved
and helped
and simply accepted me
along the way.

Contents

1

The Nature of Decision Making: Using Your Brain Effectively

Alice, in her travels through Wonderland, asked the Cheshire Cat, "Would you tell me, please, which way I ought to walk from here?" To which the Cat replied, "That depends a good deal on where you want to get to." "I don't much care where—" said Alice. "Then," said the Cat, "it doesn't matter which way you walk."

And, in all likelihood, that's your problem too; in fact, that may even be why you're reading this right now. For there are many situations in life that require decisions; they continually and constantly face you, and force you to an answer. And, too often, you don't know what to do, or why; the tension mounts and the anxiety can become unbearable. Help in making these decisions is what you want, what you are searching for, just as Alice was.

Obviously, however, you recognize that something is lacking; that in the quest for a "where" (read, instead, a richer, happier, more fulfilling life), all you need is that one little bit more and you will make it. That's why each new book, each new theory that comes along, is hailed and hosannaed; hopefully it will be the final, definitive answer.

So you buy these books, take these therapies, and attend the lectures, and often they do help you to know what you want at the moment; they do get you in touch with your feelings. But they don't tell you *how* to satisfy these needs fully, *how* to make the decisions that count—especially over the longer period of time. Generally these are battlefield therapies: they may get you through the day comparatively whole, or at least relatively unscarred, but they don't really help you with the decisions of the morrow. Or, especially, the next day. . . .

But it's not another therapy nor a new messiah that you need; unfortunately, they only approach the same problems from a slightly different point of view. It's like serving up the same old stew, having added a few new spices, and who needs that? What you *do* need is help in acting on your feelings, and in knowing how to make decisions to implement your desires in a positive, constructive way so that you can deal more efficiently and successfully with the problems of your daily life—so that the control of your future is in your hands.

That's what this book is about: how you can best use all this knowledge of yourself, and then build on it; how you can make this self-knowledge work *for* you, not only for the present, but especially for the future, so that your life can become easier to live, and richer and fuller in the living process. Nor is this book still another of the many on finding yourself; certainly there are enough of those around. Rather, I assume you have already begun to do so; with this self-understanding as a base, I will help you know how, and when, to make better decisions. That's the ultimate purpose of this book, its very marrow.

I begin precisely where the others leave off; this, hopefully, is the last of the self-help books you buy. I will help you to use the tools that you already have: your intelligence, and your experience. And you will learn how to effectively use the two sides of your brain—the intuitive half and the logical half—so that they work together and supplement and reinforce each other. And you will learn the sequential steps that are directly involved in the decision-making process so that you can be sure that you are properly using each and every step to your advantage. In short, you will learn how to take control of your life, and for your own best interests, by making the wisest decisions you can. And, fortunately, it's very easy.

I know what you're up against; I was there, too. For more time than I care to remember I spent great effort in seeking . . . something. My life wasn't bad, but it wasn't so hot either—and I didn't know why it wasn't better or, in fact, if it could be better. Like Alice, I found it difficult to decide on what I wanted to do, and how I wanted to do it. And when I did make a decision, I was too often wrong. I was in an unappealing rut, with the same dull everything: friends, clothes, work, play, money (or, rather, lack of it), even an empty relationship. Simply put, I wasn't a mess, but life sure could have been more fun.

Fortunately, now it is. I function happily, freely, well. I have fewer anxieties, fewer fears. Much of my life has changed, all for the better. I live nicely, and I enjoy myself. Maybe my life is still not perfect, but it's a damn sight happier than it ever was before.

What caused this miraculous metamorphosis was a combination of two things: I learned how to get in touch with my feelings and be able to express them, and I also learned how to *act* on these feelings. Essentially, I was able to take my life into my own hands and do the things that I wanted to do for myself. I no longer was afraid of making decisions based on my own honest desires, and I stopped having stomach palpitations when I did make them. I avoided the stupid mistakes I had continually made in the past, as well as the painful frustrations that consequently followed. I stopped stagnating, and I began to think imaginatively. I found I could clarify and reorganize my thoughts in a constructive way, so that my life was positively directed instead of being allowed merely to meander.

Simply put, I learned how to feel *and* how to reason, and with these two skills I was able to make meaningful decisions for myself. While each of these abilities is tremendously important in its own right, the combination of the two is so potent, so valuable, and so rewarding, that no one can afford to be without either. Utilizing feeling without reason is a lot like trying to play a sport with one arm tied behind you: it's not easy. But that's what I had been doing for a great portion of my life, and that's what you probably are now doing too.

Law school made the difference for me. Although I was already well in touch with my feelings, I didn't know how to act on them most effectively. But in my legal training, I learned one thing above all else, and it was the most important thing I ever learned anywhere—*how* to think. How to use my brain logically, rationally, clearly. Most of all, intelligently. I learned how to make better decisions by learning how to analyze a situation, how to separate the important from the immaterial, how to distinguish the hidden meanings from their surface appearances, and then how to evaluate the pieces, put them together, and act on them in a meaningful way so that, in the end, *it all made sense.*

This principle—the question of whether or not something makes sense—became my golden rule, branded on my brain so as never to be forgotten. And it's worth not only repeating but also making the only solid caps in this book:

DOES IT MAKE SENSE?

That's what we are rarely taught: how to think logically and critically and discriminatingly. That's what law school taught me. And that's what I'm going to help you learn.

The essential question most clients bring to their lawyers is, "What should I do?" More often than not, it isn't a legal matter but rather a personal problem for which they need help: help in organizing their thoughts, recognizing their real goals, and making the right decisions to achieve them. However, most of us lawyers charge more than our clients can afford to spend on their constant daily problems. But wouldn't it be great if you could have the benefit of a lawyer's logical training and ability in analyzing matters to help you in your decisions? Wouldn't it make life a lot easier if you could take advantage of this intelligence to help you throughout the day? Wouldn't you like to learn to think the same way? Well, that's the direction I hope to give you here.

I do not mean to imply that after reading this book you will be prepared to practice law; the Attorney General in your state might not look favorably on that. But I assure you that you will be able to think more clearly, more logically, and more intelligently about your problems and the decisions they require. And you will be able, more often than not (and certainly more often than you presently are doing), to know what you should do and how to do it effectively.

For example, I know of a young fellow who came home from one of those marathon "therapeutic" weekends, all full of whatever they fill you with. He just knew what he wanted; he recognized what he had been putting up with in his life, which he now believed was not enough; in his training he had "got it" and was now going to "take responsibility" for himself. Monday morning, bright and early, he went in to his boss to tell this unaware creature where it was all at. Poor soul: he not only expressed his feelings, honestly and fully, he also lost his job. That's my point: certainly you have to know what you want, but just as surely you also have to know the how of achieving it.

I will give you another combination to work with, too: I will help you to better use both sides of your brain. I know this sounds somewhat strange, but actually there are two sides of the brain, and we do not use both effectively. This is an area of knowledge that, until recently, was confused by phrenologists and other quacks; what is now being learned is tremendously exciting and suggests seemingly unbelievable possibilities in brain use that are almost—pardon the pun—mind-boggling.

Just to whet your appetite for what I'll go into later on, here's one small fact that will indicate the scope of this matter and suggest how incredibly well-engineered our brains are. Scientists have known for a long time that the human brain is biologically divided into two distinct halves—a right hemisphere and a left hemisphere. Connecting these two hemispheres, in effect serving as the brain's intercommunication system between its two parts, is a bundle of fibers called the corpus callosum. Okay, brace yourself: the fact is that this corpus callosum in your head consists of over two hundred million individual fibers, and each of these carries about twenty impulses a second from one hemisphere to the other! Four billion a second! It's enough to give you a headache. . . .

We have also known for some time that the right hemisphere governs the movements of the left side of the body, while the left half governs the right side. It is further recognized that the two hemispheres differ in other fundamental ways as well, and there is now substantial evidence that they function in a very specialized manner in the thinking process. Generally (some left-handed people excepted), the right side of the brain is the intuitive part, the impressionistic and relational half that has an overall, simultaneous comprehension of a problem and how to deal with it. It is holistic, and spatial. Its decisions are sometimes called "gut feelings" or "hunches"; these words are euphemisms for the proper work product of this side of the brain, merely doing its intended function. The left side of the brain is the rational part, analytical and specific, more capable of coping with problems on a logically ordered basis. It is linear, and sequential, and verbally oriented. This is where our decisions based on "good judgment" are normally made.

The importance of this information is that although we *do* use both sides of our brain, each of us has one side better developed for certain functions than the other; this dominance affects the way we think and, of course, the way we act. Neither side is better or worse than the other; they're just very different in the way they function. And we're not sure if this was biologically intended or if it is the result of a selective training process that occurs in each of us as we grow. We do know, however, that we have not properly taken advantage of this specialization in our educational methods or our developmental growth; we do not effectively use both sides of our brain conjunctively in our learning and thinking processes.

I will show you some ways that you can better use the rich potential of the brain's specialization; you can easily learn them for yourself without tools or equipment of any kind. Most importantly, with this knowledge you can then use both hemispheres of your brain and their specializations to constantly complement, supplement, and corroborate one another in your daily life. This in turn virtually guarantees that you will make better decisions more easily and more often.

The subject of how to make good decisions is not new. Literally hundreds of books have been written dealing with the process. But most of them are directed toward management men, or the military hierarchy, or other top-level wheelers and dealers of industry and politics; all these books, without exception, are totally, pompously incomprehensible. None of them work practically for you or for me in our daily living—which, after all, is of paramount importance to every one of us. Nor do any of them even vaguely consider the subjective matter of our feelings. Invariably, they address themselves to matters of such significance as deciding how many pieces of pipe a plant should make, the price at which a particular item should sell, which shades of lipstick should be dropped from the line next year. Really momentous questions. . . . But how to live a better, happier life, free of some of the frustrations and anxieties and irritations that constantly occur for all of us, is not in their ken. They would train you for a specialization that usually is of no intrinsic value to anyone and, even in the context of their own inflated egos, is at best a plush-lined rut. But for you as a *person*, nothing.

That's how this book is different: I will help you learn how to think about *living*. You will learn how to use your brain—both sides—more effectively in your daily functions, so that it is you who controls your own life, your own destiny. For your decisions are made all the time, even without your conscious recognition of them. But you must become aware of *all* your decisions; that's one of the major steps in making good ones. You must become fully aware of the problems that you should do something about. Then, you must be aware of what you actually are *doing* about these problems, and you must be equally aware of what you are *not* doing to alleviate them. And you must become aware of how much more you *can* do about them, so that you can make the conscious choice as to how much you *want* to do about them. In short, awareness is all-important: knowing what you are, and what the reality is in the conditions about you, and what you're doing about it can make all the difference in the world.

You must also be aware of what others are doing to you to create or compound these problems, so that you can effectively deal with these situations before they become massive and oppressive. Recognizing how others try to manipulate or twist the facts to suit themselves can protect and prevent you from being a pawn in their game; life is infinitely more fun when you play by your rules.

For example, I was once writing a book with another man, who had given me certain commitments in terms of the amount of time he was going to spend working on it. However, he soon began to be somewhat lax about this, and made one excuse after another as to why he was not keeping his obligations. One day, after he once again missed a fairly important session with me, and without even the courtesy of a call to let me know that he would not make it, I confronted him with this problem.

"You know, Bruce," he said, "I've always wanted to work on a book, and I very much want to do this one. I don't mean to continually disappoint you, and it is totally unintentional on my part. I just don't realize."

It was then that I decided to end the relationship, for I knew I would be in deep trouble if I tried to go on working with him. In effect, he was telling me that he was not in control of his own behavior, and that he had no awareness of doing things which resulted in my being hurt and disappointed. The only other possibility was that he *was* aware of what he was doing, and therefore was lying to me about his actions. Either way, if I allowed the relationship to endure, I would be in trouble. And I was not willing to work with a man who was either a liar or so oblivious to my feelings that these inconsiderate acts would certainly continue in spite of his assurances, especially since he was not in control of them.

This is the kind of awareness I will be talking about. You will recognize the situations you are in; you will clearly see what other people actually *are* doing to you, and not merely what they want you to *think* they are doing. Further, you will know what you can do about their manipulation. Then, with this awareness, and with the skills and abilities that you will also learn, you will make those decisions that will guarantee that you are in control of your life and not subject to other people's domination of it in any way. You will *never* allow the hurts to continue because of your inaction or your lack of awareness.

This book will help you to find this awareness—of the answers that are there, but are sometimes elusive, or deceiving, or unable to be pinned down. And I keep using the word "help," for I shall be very supportive; I know I would have welcomed such help before I knew how to find the answers. I promise you that you will be better able to decide *what* you want to do, *how* you will do it, and *when* you should do it. And I can easily demonstrate that it is very well worth the effort, and that it can be done. The proof is simple: if your own feelings of inadequacy in this area don't convince you, look around at people you know, people who, by *your* standards—not anyone else's—are the happy and successful ones. Invariably, you will see someone who knows how to think, and how to decide.

Doesn't it make sense?

2

Decisions:
What They Are

A decision may be defined in several ways. The definition I like best is this: a decision is the timely choice or selection of a future course of action. This statement says several things, and it says them simply and clearly. It assumes that you want, or need, to make a choice; there is a problem to be solved, some matter to be determined. It suggests that various alternatives are available from which you can choose; that there are, in fact, several viable courses of action open to you. It declares a deliberate determination on your part, rather than a passive acceptance of things happening *to* you. It implies that purposive motivation governs your choice; that you make your decisions on the basis of what *you* want for *yourself*. Finally, it presumes your performing the course of action decided upon—and at the optimum moment in time.

Actually, you go through this process of selection and determination hundreds of times a day, whether you want to or not, and whether you are aware of it or not. You cannot avoid it: *everything* you do is the end result of a decision, either one that was made in the past (and you are now merely repeating and reaffirming) or one that you must make, consciously and deliberately, now when it is necessary. Decisions are required in every aspect of your life; they concern emotional and practical matters ranging in importance from the most mundane to the most significant. And some decisions, from time to time, are even on the crisis level; there are pivotal moments when the whole future course of your life is determined by the immediate choice you make.

Of course, the relative importance of the matters to be decided varies with all people. I know a man who breaks into a cold sweat over as simple a decision (to others) as what tie to wear; however, he can casually and without qualms invest thousands of dollars during a short phone call to his broker. Others have trouble deciding on relationships: who to go out with (or not); who to bed with (and when); how deep the involvement should be, if at all; if it should be continued, or ended. There are decisions of career, of family, of children's upbringing, of religious training, of saving or spending. There are deeply personal matters, such as whether or not to use a birth-control method and, if so, what kind. These—and there are myriad others—are all life decisions, each one deeply important at the time to the person making it. And all these problems take energy to solve; generally more than they are worth and, even worse, often more than is necessary.

Most of our decisions, however, are habitual; having once been made they become ingrained and receive no thought. The consequences are usually predictable and generally not of great moment. Presumably at some time long past you considered the matter, you arrived at a solution, and the situation became routinized. It is safe: what has been accepted in the past can continue in the future. And it is easy: what has already been decided requires no further work or effort. The method and route of travel we use from home to office is one example of such inertia; it is a programmed act. Probably once upon a time, when we were first faced with the problem, we thought out the best way to go. We might even have tried several alternatives. Finally, and most likely with not too much thought, we decided on one course, possibly because it was quicker, or cheapest, or had the most attractive people to stare at. For whatever reason, that was our choice, and we haven't thought about it since. We just go that way.

The places where we shop or the foods that we eat are almost as fixed. Our daily chores, the friends that we see, the social activities in which we participate are all similarly habitualized and repeated. We continue these patterns as we always have: without concern, and without great care. And unless and until any of these acts are again pondered, they will remain on this unthinking level, possibly forever.

We pay even less conscious attention to our reflexive actions; we perform some of them so automatically, and so without thought, that they seem to be part of the subconscious. Which, in actual fact, is what they are; they are decisions that you continually make with your right brain, and some of them can be vital. For example, while you are driving your car you constantly act and react in split-seconds, with your very life depending on many of these instantaneous decisions. Trying to run across a street in a hurry, against both the light and traffic, is a similar situation. You cope with such situations reflexively, almost haphazardly, and invariably without conscious thought. And although they *are* decisions that you constantly make, there is little I can say about them other than to express my hope that both your patron saints and your animal instincts for survival are not taking the day off. (If you wish information on these risks, I refer you to any good insurance agent.) However, I *will* discuss some of the decisions that seem to be reflexive, such as sudden bursts of temper or hostility, for these often get us into trouble that we really can avoid.

What I am more concerned with, and what is to be the major area of concentration of this book—because this is what most concerns you—is the deliberative level of decision making. This involves by far the most difficult problems we face, the ones that give us the most trouble in our attempts to resolve them well and successfully. Generally these are matters that are of more importance to our overall sense of happiness and well-being than those we deal with on the habitual level; consequently they require more care in the making, even though they may not be as vital as some of those on the reflexive level that I've already mentioned. Invariably, there is a conscious need to make a choice: some problem must be dealt with; some matter must be determined.

This need to decide on a course of action may be one that is thrust upon us by external events, or it may arise from some problem or uncertainty that we are personally aware of and wish to ameliorate. The fellow who was fired from his job was forced to deal with this fact and decide what to do; life goes on and the bills come in. At the same time, another man I know chose to leave his job for reasons that were of importance to him. Both these men, however, are now in the same situation: unemployed, and with the immediate need to decide what to do.

In all likelihood the man who chose to leave his job had done a good deal of preparation in coming to this decision and had also thought ahead as to his course of action; but the one who was fired obviously did not have such an opportunity, since his decision to speak up had been hasty and ill-conceived. However, the fact is that at this moment both men are in the same decision-making position, even though for different reasons. Both must think consciously, carefully, and hard about what they are now going to do.

Similarly, the woman who decides that her relationship with the man she is living with should be over now faces the same problem that another woman, who is told by her man that it *is* over, also must deal with: what do I do now? A deliberate effort must be made by each of these people to resolve the problem. And to resolve it well.

Because so much is at stake in some of these situations, we often do not make a decision *when* it is necessary because we fear we will make a mistake. We want to be *sure*, and so we procrastinate. Frequently we find it much easier to avoid our problems than to decide how to deal with them—or, at least, it seems so. But you should recognize the simple fact that a decision, as well as its effectuation, is made and done just as definitely and just as deliberately by the *inaction* as it would have been by the doing of a specific thing. The person who says "I'll think about it tomorrow" or "I'll worry about it later" has in reality *made* a decision. His hesitation and uncertainty have led to a continuation of the status quo; he has actually chosen to go along with the situation he is presently in. But he would die before he'd ever admit this; at all costs he must maintain the facade of a wise, deliberative person. And in most cases the delusion is honest. Such people really believe that they are not condoning inaction, but are instead contemplating some future action.

For example, several couples I know are in bad relationships that are causing them much grief and misery; it is a fair assumption that they would be happier apart. But, whatever their reasons (which I'll discuss later), they are allowing these relationships to continue, putting off the moment of truth for a "little" while. Actually they have not delayed the decision, but rather have chosen to avoid the confrontation. They *have* decided, and responsibility for this act of avoidance follows as a direct consequence as certainly as if they had chosen divorce.

Similarly, I know a man who is unhappy in his job; he is "thinking" of leaving and finding another. I know a woman who is "thinking" of getting a job, since she is tired of being a housewife. I know a student who is "thinking" of changing her major because she is not sure that the field she is in really interests her. I know a woman who is "thinking" of cutting her hair and styling it differently. I know another who is "thinking" about moving to the West Coast from New York.

Interestingly, all these people have one thing in common—each has been "thinking" about his or her particular dream for the last several months; each has continually expressed doubts and reservations about the present situation; and each has said that he or she is going to do something to change it. However, none of them has. Sadly, these people have chosen (through inaction) to remain in their present situations, although they are foolishly trying to maintain (if only to themselves) the illusion of intelligent deliberation. And they delude themselves into thinking that they have not yet made a decision and there is still time to do so.

This, of a certainty, will only be regretted. The poet's phrase is unhappily, too often true: "For all the sad words of tongue and pen, the saddest are these: 'It might have been!' " Of course, these people can always change their minds and at some later time decide on another course of action, but my point is that, for this moment at least, they *have* made a decision even though they prefer to believe they have not yet done so.

There are other people who *are* aware they are making their decisions by default—and still they do nothing about it. They, unlike those who are still "thinking" (and vegetating), do realize that they are not "doing something." But they are overcome by the problem, or fear the possible consequences of a decision, or get so mired in it for one reason or another (which I will also go into in great detail) that they *won't* act. They *can* act, but will not—and I use these words advisedly.

A friend of mine, talking about her love life, told me that "I get so bogged down with the possibilities of what might be that I don't do the things that I really want to do." Then she paused, sadly, for she's very smart and realized what she was leading up to: "But that's doing something—getting bogged down—so I can't say I'm not doing anything. I *am* doing something: *nothing.*"

This woman is an active, vital person, very successful in her career, but not so happy in her relationships, which was bothering her. And she recognized this anxiety as being the result of her own inability to act, for she later said that she hated herself for this; since she felt that she had no control over her life, she was not effecting any change for progress. As she put it, "There are no dynamics in my life. And it's my fault, because I'm not doing anything. And I'd *rather* do it, even make a mistake, and deal with the consequences." This woman is also typical: aware of her problems, aware that she is doing nothing about them, and aware that she is the one who is compounding her own frustration. Yet she is unable to take that positive step of action that will resolve her dilemma.

Then there are others who avoid decisions by taking actions that actually are not relevant to the real, underlying situation. Yet they delude themselves into thinking that by doing something they are dealing with their problem; in fact they are doing nothing about the matter that must be dealt with. In effect, it is again making a decision by inaction, even though the avoidance may be masked by an expenditure of energy in some other direction.

I am a perfect case in point. I was in an unhappy marriage, one destined for divorce. But because I was unwilling or unable to deal with it at that time, I put off the problem by doing something that was totally unrelated. I went to law school; the concentration this required temporarily allowed me the luxury of not dealing with the horror that was home. Nor did I even have to "think" about the relationship. But all I really did was postpone the moment of truth by my inaction; the problems of the marriage were still there, even exacerbated, when I graduated. All that I did with this charade was to poorly veil my real act of cowardice, and only for a short interlude at that. And although I could have indefinitely continued the unconscious decision to do nothing about the marriage, I had learned at law school how to think more clearly than before, and I was soon able to come to grips with what had to be done.

Sometimes, of course, you can get lucky, and make the right choice by chance, without any awareness of your real needs. This is what I did by going to law school which, fortunately, turned out very successfully. But you can't depend on luck; gamblers—good ones, at least—*always* play the percentages. In Las Vegas, where more money is made by the casino owners than by most of our giant corporations, they say that "luck is for losers." You *can* get lucky but you can't—and certainly shouldn't—count on it, or even look for it. You're gambling on the biggest chance-board of all: your life. You gamble on love, career, and friends; you put a certain part of yourself on the line every time you do *anything*. So what you should do is what the successful gamblers do: bet on as sure a thing as you can. Simply put, get the probabilities in your favor; work *with* the odds and not against them. Make your own "luck": learn to recognize what you want to do, and how, and why. Learn to make better decisions, more of the time.

What are "better" decisions? Well, on a corporate level the criterion of success is usually sufficiently simple: profits. On a personal level it is not. Each of us is unique; you and I have our own special needs and desires and values, and these are very personal and very private matters. What represents "success" to you may not be desirable or, possibly, even acceptable to others. "Success" has different meanings for different people; the only way it can really be measured is the degree to which you accomplish that which you set out to do. Further, "success" is often ephemeral; what may seem to you to be crucially important may merely be so at the time, momentarily serving certain needs until they are replaced by newer, more pressing wants. Therefore, measurement of your personal satisfaction requires that, unlike Alice, you constantly know as you move through life where you want to go, what you want to do.

That's the crux of good decision making: your decisions should be *yours*, based on *your* wants and needs and desires. And they must also be based on *your* values and *your* moral code, not mine or anyone else's. Provided only that you properly respect the rights of others, I subscribe fully to Ernest Hemingway's philosophy: "What's moral is what you feel good after. What's immoral is what you feel bad after." Therefore, since it is your life and your feelings, it must also be your values that determine your decisions, not anyone else's. As for me, I shall try not to offer any judgmental evaluation of any kind; it is you who must decide.

In this regard, you must also recognize the fact that not only people but even cultures bring their personal climates of opinion to bear upon this matter; therefore you must be prepared—and able—to fend off all these pressures and set your own personal and individual values if you wish to make the wisest and best decisions for yourself. Choose what *you* want to do, not what your society tells you to do. The classic story to illustrate this is that of the man far from shore in a sinking boat with his wife, his mother, and his child. Only the man knows how to swim, and he himself can do so barely well enough to save only one of the others. If you were he, who would you rescue?

In Western cultures, the answer almost always is the child. But in Eastern societies, it is as invariably the mother; their rationale is that both the wife and the child can be replaced, but not the mother. Clearly, the particular cultural background, the different ethnic teachings, all enter and control. Consequently, you must try to recognize and separate your private and personal beliefs from those you have merely been conditioned to hold; it is imperative that you think of what you want for yourself. You must constantly be wary of external pressures that may influence your decisions. For example, it is revealing to note that if the question of who to save is asked of Western men when their wives are present, the proportion of those who would choose their wives markedly increases over those who are asked the question in private. It seems obvious that the presence of someone to whom you are beholden in some fashion can easily affect the value judgment—and decision—that you make. Therefore it is vital that you are sure the values you choose are truly yours, rather than what you feel compelled to think they *should* be. For it is these personal values that determine your life.

You must also realize that decisions are not ends in themselves; they are merely steps—even milestones—in the course of our lives. Each decision, no matter how minor or major, is but the introduction to the next question. Each is a necessary progression in life; all are irrevocably intertwined and interrelated. Remember the man who left his job? In fact, he made—and acted upon—a deliberate decision to do so; this in turn led to the need for his next decision as to what to do with his life. And the man who decided to speak up to his boss is in the same position. The directions each must then decide upon are countless: possibly a different career, a "better" job in the same field, a vacation, his own business, or whatever. Having decided this, he must then make the consequent decisions that this choice determines. On, and on, and on.

All decisions are like this: sequential, and cumulative; each succeeding one builds upon the previous many, and there is no end to the process. There are no beginnings, and there are no ends; for that kind of tidiness you should go to a film. Decisions are the structure of life, and they continue throughout life. One affects the next, even if in only a small way; the outcome of today's decisions lead to, possibly bring on, and certainly influence tomorrow's problems, and consequently the future need for more decisions.

And rarely, if ever, are decisions finalities, nor should they be approached or treated with that kind of reverence. Decisions *can* be changed or modified; the only valid constant *is* change. What is now decided need remain so only until a better way is found; this is the only verity, and simply means that you're smarter today than you were yesterday. Shortly after he was nominated, Jimmy Carter said, in answer to a reporter's question, "I do not intend to be bound by absolute consistency. I reserve the right to learn and to change my mind as I go along." Flexibility is a sign of intelligence and practicality, and it's also a mark of courage. Even more, the ability to think about what you have done, to examine it and re-evaluate it, is a sign of personal and mental maturity.

To recognize that you have now changed in your values, or that the basis on which you made an earlier decision is no longer pertinent or, possibly, valid, is merely to realize that you have grown. So be willing, when necessary, to revise your thinking and change your mind. Life is too short to continue to live a mistake; if the time has arrived when what you are doing (which was determined by an earlier decision) is now no longer the right direction for you, allowing it to continue is merely to accept the status quo because of your inaction—and we've already gone through the evils of that!

Some people think it is wrong to change their minds; they consider it weakness, or vacillation, or an inability to really decide. I don't agree; I think this view is narrow-minded and even demeaning. I am wary of the man who says, especially with pride, "I never change my mind." Either he's a liar or a fool, and I am frightened of both. Certainly he's in a rut. He knows, and will proudly tell you, that he's a rock, a man you can depend on and trust; you can, but not to think. Unyielding stubbornness, masquerading under the name of consistency, is the hobgoblin of little minds and demonstrates nothing quite as much as a lack of imagination and intelligence.

Take marriage as a decision, for example. The vows, and the intent, and the commitment all suggest and even demand permanence; most people entering matrimony accept and want this condition as an integral basis of the relationship. Yet the statistics, even though they are shocking and appalling, tell us something else: today, more than one out of every three marriages ends in divorce. Therefore, you must approach even as momentous a decision as this with an air of reality. You should not expect or anticipate a divorce, nor should you enter marriage with any such reservations. But you should be aware that if the relationship does turn sour, or if either of you changes to such an extent as you grow and develop that the marriage no longer makes sense, you are not trapped forever because of the earlier decision.

I know of two lovely people who had a beautiful affair through college and a very fulfilling marriage thereafter. But then they began to move in different directions and no longer shared the same interests to the same degree they had when younger. The divergence grew, and so did the separation of their emotional involvement; they found that they were each developing other relationships that were becoming more meaningful than the one they were in. Fortunately, too, it happened for both of them at about the same time, so there was no hostility or recriminating scenes; they were able to handle this growth as mature people should. They accepted the fact that their marriage was over; they got an amicable divorce and are now still quite friendly, even though no longer lovers.

Divorces do have a valid purpose; if you go this route there should be no guilt, or shame, or embarrassment. There should be no regrets; presumably much was gained and shared, and the experience was vital and worthwhile for the time it lasted. The memory should be of the good things, not the bad. The hope—and belief—should be that each decision was valid when made; now each person should go on—positively—with life, making new and better decisions. And as we grow in all things, not only marriage, our decisions must grow with us.

The point is that you should not underestimate the complexity of the problem of making a good decision; expect—and accept— some inevitable failures. We all make mistakes from time to time, for we're human. Obviously, if we could always be certain of the consequences of our choice, we would have no worries of any kind, and there would be no reason for this book. And the outcome is always unpredictable, as it is beyond our power to control. External events and other people constantly enter into the equation, complicating it and making the result less than certain. Because of this, we can't win all the time; this is a fantasy that you cannot expect to occur.

But you *do* control yourself, and so what you must do is learn to guide and shape your decisions, and determine your course of action, in such a way that you have as good a chance as possible to influence the outcome and have it turn out as you wish. And don't be upset when a decision turns out to be bad; learn from it, if you can. Try to discover what went wrong and then try to avoid the same error in your thinking or judgment in the future. The cliché is valid; learn from your mistakes. And then be willing—and prepared—to correct them.

Now I would like to say a few words about how this book is organized. But first a small digression is in order: I must apologize, and hereby do, to all those who are offended by my not continually using the feminine pronoun as well as the masculine; you must realize that it would be awkward to constantly say "his or her" in this discussion. And our language has no satisfactory substitute other than "this person," which only works part of the time and usually badly at that. So throughout the rest of the book please substitute for yourself if you wish; whenever I say "his" or "him" or "he," use whichever pronoun you prefer.

It is important that you realize that the procedure in making a decision is usually a homogeneous one; the "steps" are neither sharply delineated nor can they be conveniently compartmentalized. In practice the elements run together like a flowing river. However, in order to make the overall procedure as comprehensible as possible, I am going to break it down into segments that are admittedly artificial. I'll elaborate extensively on each of these elements in turn, and I'll offer suggestions on how you can best perform them rapidly, easily, practically, and effectively. I'll give you warning signals so that you will be able to tell when things are going wrong, and shortcuts to help you make them go right, or at least faster. In this way you will have the knowledge and ability to determine which individual aspect of this total process may be giving you trouble. The decision-making process is the sum total of its parts; improving each part can only result in better decisions.

Since I think it will help you in your use of this book to have an overall view and understanding of the total concept of making a decision before you begin to examine it in detail, I'd like to briefly summarize all the components that go into the process. This will give you the broad picture so that you can keep the individual elements in perspective as we deal with each.

Obviously, you can never really deal with a problem unless and until you have a basic knowledge of your pertinent goals, both long and short range, for it is these objectives that are the meaning of your life. They give it perspective, and dimension, and quality. These goals are the standard against which you must recognize and evaluate your problems; your goals must ultimately guide, shape, and determine your course of action. Therefore, an understanding of your goals—and any reasons there may be for difficulty in setting them—is probably more critical and of more importance to your success and your happiness than any other step in the decision-making process.

You must also recognize that a problem exists and that a decision, which you cannot avoid, is required. This perception is sometimes easy: the poor guy who was fired for having told off his boss immediately knew what he had to contend with. More often, however, the need for a decision is not this obvious, and an awareness of the existence of a problem is frequently blocked from the mind. The realization that an issue exists and that you must examine it, and explore it, and consciously deal with it is all-important; so is an objective appraisal of the matter. You must strip away all rationalizations, all fantasy, all fear. And there must be maturity, understanding, and intelligence in your appraisal of the dimensions of the problem and, in particular, the priority it must be accorded in your life.

Knowing what you really want for yourself, and aware of the problem you face, you then can begin to determine what alternatives are available to you. You can also begin collecting all the relevant and pertinent material on each of these options that will help you in making your decision. This requisite knowledge must include an honest appraisal of your capabilities and limitations in relation to the problem; all this information will be used to advantage when you are finally making your choice.

Next comes your evaluation of these alternatives. Here you must critically examine each of them in turn, marshaling and analyzing all the information you have obtained in an attempt to predict as accurately as possible the consequences of each option. You must make a very practical, no-nonsense appraisal of the ultimate chances of achievement of your goals, while weighing the practical consideration of the risks you must take and the price you must pay.

We then come to the moment of truth—the choice and the act. What to do and (very importantly) *when* to do it. And then, to do it! This vital step—taking action—is, for some people, the hardest. But unless you make an appropriate commitment (of money, time involvement, belief, action), the whole process is for naught. You *must* make a conscious decision, and a consequent act, or you have wasted your time. Your energy and your effort have gone into the process; now you must make it all pay off.

Finally, there must be an appraisal—and constant reappraisal—of the results of your decision. You must continually ask yourself how you can improve it. You must also recognize what you have learned from it. And you must always be aware of the new problems that stem from it, and that you must now in turn also deal with.

That's it; that's the decision-making process in brief. Realize that elements overlap and that what I may say about one aspect will have just as much bearing on several others; as you make your decisions, use this material as it may pertain to each of them, and to you. And don't hesitate to question—or even challenge—what I say. Remember, these decisions are *yours*; they should not be made for you by anyone else.

You must make your decisions on the basis of your intelligence and experience, not mine. I'm not trying to convince anyone of the sanctity of my ideas. I have no "cause," I have no "theory," I have no "therapy," I have no "discipline." I have nothing to promote, except the hope—and intent—to have better-thinking people around in this world. For, after all, that's the best way I know to make it a happier world—and I live in it too. I just want to help you to think, and analyze, and decide more intelligently. I want to help you to function better, more clearly, more specifically, so that you can achieve freedom in, and control over, your own life.

That's what it's all about. It does make sense.

3

Your Two Brains—
Intuition and Logic

Unquestionably, there have been many times in your life when you made a decision for no apparent reason: it was simply a "hunch" or a "feeling" that determined the choice you made, the direction in which you went. Maybe you chose a job this way; maybe you began—or ended—a relationship. And if you were asked "Why?" you possibly felt a little foolish, even stupid, at having allowed yourself to behave in such a seemingly haphazard manner. Such doubts, when they occur, are usually compounded; probably you then became unsure of the decision, afraid you were wrong, convinced that you were a total disaster as a thinker. Certainly such a decision was not to be defended, even if it couldn't be avoided.

Yet, if you look back and evaluate the results, I'll bet that more often than not you made the right rather than the wrong decision. And the reason (there is one) is simple. Actually, your choice was not based on a whim, nor was it random chance; your decision was a valid one, and it *was* made by your brain. That is, it was made by the right half of your brain, the intuitive side that functions in this manner. The fact is that intuition is just as much a part of our brain's operation as is logic; it *is* thinking, only of a kind we have not yet learned to understand. Logic is knowledge based on rational thought; that is, by the use of reason and inference. Intuition is also knowledge, but it is instinctive and without rational thought, without specific reasons. Logic and intuition are both products of our brain's activity; both are parts of each of us.

However, since our training has always emphasized and made a demand for demonstrable proof, there is a resultant and understandable reluctance to accept the guidance of the more amorphous and intuitive side of the brain, especially since its workings are not really comprehended. But intuition can and should be part of your decision-making process. Simply because we have not learned how to use our intuition is not sufficient cause to ignore it. We need all the help we can get, and we certainly should be using our brain—our *whole* brain, not just half of it.

Let me tell you a little about the brain. I think you will find this information truly fascinating and very helpful in making better decisions. For once you know what's going on up there, you will not only be able to regularly use this intuitive side as well as the logical half when you want to, but you will also find that you are quite confident and comfortable in doing so.

Physically, the human brain is quite small: it weighs only about three pounds (less than one and a half kilos) and is roughly the size of half a grapefruit. The largest portion of the brain is the cerebrum, which controls all our mental activity, our voluntary actions, and our sensory abilities. Biologically the cerebrum is divided into two hemispheres, and there is that bundle of nerve fibers called the corpus callosum that joins them and transmits electrical impulses back and forth between them; these are somehow translated by the brain cells into usable bits of information. These impulses are brief bursts—about one-thousandth of a second, traveling at speeds ranging from one to one hundred meters per second, and occurring (you will recall) in each of the two hundred million fibers about twenty times a second. It's like a small electrical storm up there, going on all the time!

Probably the most compelling fact to be stated about the brain is that its potential is virtually unlimited; all our present research strongly suggests that we are only barely using our abilities. For, incredible as it may seem, although the brain has between ten and twenty *billion* cells, neurobiologists say that only a small portion of these appear to be utilized, possibly not even 10 percent; and even these may be only partially functioning, for *each* such cell seems to be capable of holding or controlling thousands of bits of information. We can only guess at what we could do if more (or all) of our brain was also used.

Numerous cases and experiments document individuals' performances of seemingly incredible mental feats that go beyond what are commonly thought of as "normal" bounds. For example, and on a very simplistic level, pain, hunger, heat, and cold are often referred to as "states of mind"; in fact, that's exactly what they are. And they can easily be controlled; it's simply a matter of our learning how to do this. There are people who by their thoughts can effectively raise the temperature in the fingers of one hand while at the same time lowering it in the other. Some subjects can deliberately change their heartbeat rate as well as their blood pressure. There are those who can write with both hands simultaneously, setting forth a question with one hand while giving the answer with the other. Houdini is reported to have been able to swallow a key to the locks that shackled him; then, when hidden from the audience's view, he would regurgitate it and manipulate it with his mouth to escape his bonds. Speedreading, in which whole pages of type are read and fully comprehended at a glance, is being taught even to children; there are people who can read this book (and thoroughly understand it) in less than thirty minutes.

These, obviously, are relatively simple and unsophisticated tasks. More compelling evidence of the scope of our ability is that we have invented bombs that can easily destroy our planet and devised machines that put us on another; our potential is awesome. There is no question but that our mental capacity is virtually limitless; we merely have to learn how to do what it seems very apparent we can do.

Although some of our knowledge about the brain has been available for some time, mainly because of research on brain-damaged individuals, only recently have we really made considerable advances in the area of brain function and specialization. Essentially, this new information was gained as an offshoot of surgical work done with uncontrollable epileptics; in these cases the two halves of the brain were severed in a successful attempt to diminish the intensity of the epileptic attacks. Subsequent and intensive testing on these split-brain individuals has led to the most important of our present knowledge and theories about the brain and how it functions.

At birth, the two halves of the normal brain seem to be fairly equal in potential; no specialization is apparent. But then, as the child develops, specificity does too; the two hemispheres become individually dominant for different functions. That is, each hemisphere becomes more important in the performance of a particular activity than the other; for all intents and purposes it seems to take over the control of this conduct, possibly to an almost exclusive degree. However, the opposite hemisphere is not excluded from participation in or knowledge of this function; the neural communication via the corpus callosum provides for the necessary complementary awareness and behavior.

Let me explain this by telling you of someone whose corpus callosum was severed; this of course meant that his two hemispheres could no longer share their information or transmit it each to the other. An object was placed in his left hand, out of sight of either eye. (Remember that the sensory discrimination of this hand is transmitted to the right brain.) Then he was asked what he was holding, to which he replied (his left brain speaking, since that is the area of our verbal language), "I don't know. Nothing." With no means of communication from the right brain to the left brain, he was therefore unable to tell the questioner what the right, nonverbal brain knew but the left brain had no knowledge of. However, when he was later presented with pictures of various objects, he was able to point (with his left hand, governed by the right brain which had this visual information) to the object he had been holding earlier.

In the normal person, with his brain intact, both hemispheres are continually, constantly working and sharing their information; always remember that it is not left versus right, it is left *plus* right. Nonetheless, what does seem to happen is that at any given moment one or the other side is dominant, depending on the primary activity of the brain. And, although this does not mean that either side is more important, in some people there does seem to be a tendency to favor one side more than the other—that is, to use it more often than the other. Lawyers, architects, scientists, and mathematicians are primarily left-brain people. Artists, actors, musicians are just as definitely the opposite. Further, it now seems certain that although these two hemispheres constantly complement each other there is an independence and a specialization in the way that they perform, with this dichotomy so marked in its effects that we can accurately refer to each hemisphere as if it's a separate brain by itself.

In right-handed people (about 90 percent of the population) the left hemisphere of the brain is the one in which the verbal, logical, analytical functions are predominantly located. It is the side of reason. This side of the brain thinks explicitly, sequentially, intellectually; in doing so it uses language that has meaning and ideas that take concrete form. In Freudian terms, it is the *conscious*. It seems to work in a linear way—that is, it progresses in logical steps from one point to the next, *a* to *b* to *c*. It puts words together to communicate; I have written this book with my left brain, and you are receiving it in yours.

The left brain can take apart an idea, separate it into its many pieces, and examine each one individually and in all its ramifications before putting it back together again, often in a more rational and systematized way. It is very ordered, very focused, very specific and precise; it has a definite sense of sequence and time that can even border on compulsiveness. When the left brain is doing its job properly, everything is clearly thought out, everything has its reason, everything can be explained.

The right side of the brain is pretty much the opposite, at least in function. This side is intuitive, spontaneous, and receptive; it perceives and grasps an entire situation at once, impressionistically as well as spatially and holistically. It is the side that thinks in visual images and feelings and has very little, if any, language; for all intents and purposes it is speechless and illiterate, almost mute, like a primitive yet very intelligent animal. It has its own way of knowing, which is neither verbal nor linear and which we barely understand; it processes information implicitly, in an overall, instantaneous, visual way, and with no sense of time. You're never quite sure which part of the thought came first; it's as if the whole idea occurred at once, simultaneously and seemingly almost spontaneously, just as it does in our dreams—which are also a right-brain activity.

It is in this intuitive side of the brain, and not in our stomachs, that we get our feelings, our "hunches," our "gut reactions." The right side is our emotional side, very open to people while almost sensuously diffuse in its approach to details; a Haiku poem well describes its way of functioning: "Today I met a stranger whom I knew a thousand years." The right brain is probably the hiding ground for our primeval fears and our psychological hangups; again in Freudian terms it is our *unconscious*, our introspective side. And it is primarily responsible for our aesthetic responses and our artistic accomplishment; "inspiration" and "taste" are purely right-brain functions. The right brain may not know anything in the verbal, literate sense, but it may easily know *everything* in the spatial, intuitive, and creative sense. Einstein said of himself: "A thought comes, and I may try to express it in words afterwards." Essentially, the right brain is our imagination, our intuition, and our instinct. Its functions can only be felt, not explained.

If you're left-handed you are not necessarily the direct reverse of this in the way you function. The indication is that about two-thirds of left-handed people have the same brain orientation as right-handers, and the remaining one-third are either the direct opposite of this or may be somewhat less specialized. However, since the practical effect in the way the brain is used for our thinking and decisions is the same for all of us, no matter what the handedness, for the balance of this discussion I'm going to disregard the question. Obviously, it's irrelevant; all that really matters is that you recognize that there is a distinction between the intuitive and the logical sides, and that you learn how to use this information so it can be of value to you in making your decisions.

In particular, and even though we may not understand the how of our intuitive right-brain kind of thinking, we must welcome it with the dignity and respect it deserves rather than dismiss and demean it. We must realize that our instantaneous reactions to a situation or a problem, our instinctive awareness of the essence of a matter and its ultimate outcome which we have always referred to as our "gut feelings," are in fact true products of our brain's activity and not merely visceral rumblings. These attitudes, these hunches, these judgments that we grasp in a flash—without having reasons for them or knowing their logical *why?*—are the result of all our years of experience, together with all our instantaneous and immediate perceptions, and are without doubt a very important and valid part of our conceptual processes.

Decisions off the top of our heads are actually based on this inner intelligence, and so they should—and must—be given credence and taken advantage of. But, unfortunately, too often we ignore these feelings, these flashes of instinct and intuition. Too frequently we do not give sufficient heed to these insights and these perceptions. And when we dismiss these thoughts, we lose; the price we pay is enormous, and could easily be avoided. Understand, of course, that I'm not talking about the wild hopes and speculative fantasies that some people mistakenly call "hunches"; impulsively buying stock because you're "sure" you're going to make a killing usually will murder nothing but your bank account. Obviously you must (logically or intuitively) differentiate between what is only wishful desire and a true sense of cognition and instinctive understanding; hope alone is *not* the proper kind of feeling to depend on.

It may be that we do not readily accept the guidance of our right brain precisely because the working of the intuitive mind is not really understood; its powers cannot be analyzed, or measured, or broken down into steps. But that is its essence, and its strength: it *is* instinctive, emotional, creative, simultaneous. It can only be thought of in an overall concept, not in ordered parts. Paradoxically, the only way we can describe the activity of the intuitive side of the brain, which has almost no verbal function of its own, is to try to comprehend and conceptualize it through the other side of the brain—the logical, verbal half. That's exactly what I'm doing now, by trying to explain intuition in words, and that's how you're receiving this information. But you probably have already had that momentary flash of intuitive, right-brain feeling: you know exactly what I am talking about; in fact you always knew it.

Western society has concentrated on educating the left, or logical, brain. We have reduced the indicia of intelligence to what can be taught—and measured—verbally; we evaluate it on the basis of a structured and ordered pattern. Of course, to a great extent this is due to nature: our daily lives are linear, with a past, present, and future, one event following another. For whatever the cause, we are a society of specialists, of highly refined thinkers. We applaud analysis, we treasure reason. And although our artists are extolled, this is almost the exception and not the rule; in terms of our general education the arts are really tacked on to the curriculum, almost as an afterthought. (Even there, most of them are verbally, not spatially, oriented.) The fact is that we want our lives, and our training, to be spelled out and to be compartmentalized neatly so that we can define, and understand, and explain. Order is easier.

I am not suggesting that placing such significant valuation on reason is inherently wrong; I'd be out of business if logic went out of style. Rather, I deplore the fact that the intuitive side of the brain is ignored in our training and dismissed in our lives. And it is this lack that we must now correct if we are to think clearly and decide well.

Probably because this concept of right-brain thinking is so new and no one really comprehends it that it is not taught in our schools; it is hard to explain what is not understood. And if right-brain thinking should inadvertently or spontaneously appear, its use is generally neither accepted nor appreciated; even worse, it usually is actually discouraged. I heard a story about a young girl in elementary school who, along with her classmates, was given the assignment of describing a spring rainstorm. When her turn came to recite, she instead walked over to a piano in the corner of the room and ingenuously proceeded to give a musical interpretation based on her feelings of this event. Unfortunately, her literal-minded teacher sent a stifling note home to the girl's parents, terming her actions "brazen." Obviously this girl was thinking—and creating—with her intuitive side, and this should have been praised by all concerned instead of being a disgrace.

It is this same tendency to take a limited view of life's problems that we must remedy so as to avoid stupid, possibly dangerous decisions outside the school as well. One such piece of near-disaster recently occurred on the West Coast; a group of marvelously talented artisans was attracting progressively heavier weekend traffic to their small town from nearby San Francisco. The local transportation experts, "logically" fixated to a fault and armed with tons of computerized projections, decided that a new road would have to be built in order to handle the constantly increasing flow of cars. Of course—and wouldn't you guess?—the planned highway required the condemnation of most of the houses and barns in which the craftsmen were living and working. (It's the old story: the symptom was cured; it's just too bad the patient died.) Fortunately, the mayor of the town—himself one of the artists and intuitively oriented—realized that, with the attraction of the talent gone, new roads would no longer be needed, and was able to abort the highway plan in time.

This story aptly illustrates the point I'm making: we unquestioningly are designed to use both sides of our brain to think and to make decisions; therefore we cannot allow or expect one side or the other to continually go it alone. We have this beautifully engineered mechanism to do our bidding and to help keep us from trouble; we should take full advantage of it and allow it to properly function for us. We must both think and feel; each side must help and build on and with the other. When this happens, a synergistic effect seems to take place—that is, the overall and aggregate effect of the two sides working together is larger and more comprehensive than the mere sum of the two sides. It's as if something extra is added, something beyond that which each side has contributed individually: a relationship occurs when they combine. The process is comparable to the kind of marriage that happens when two gases such as hydrogen and oxygen combine to form water, or atoms fuse, to make energy. Or a man and woman do, to create a child. Similarly, this coming together of the two parts of the brain may be what we know as "inspiration" and "creativity"; after all, what *does* happen up there in our heads? Whatever this miracle is, go with it, and as far as you can.

Therefore, each side of the brain must be allowed and encouraged to contribute to, and share in, the decision-making process. Each side must be given its due, its full measure of credence and respect. And each side must be used to complement and supplement and reinforce the other. In addition, and in effect, this acts as an invaluable system of checks and balances, a method of review and reinforcement. Each side of your brain should initiate ideas; each side should oversee and corroborate the thoughts of the other; each side should correct and temper the oversights or excesses or mistakes of the other. Both sides of your brain must be in harmony and must agree each with the other if you want to be absolutely sure your decision is right. If your decision "feels" wrong, or both sides are not really in synch, beware! Only when you have the feeling of peace and serenity that comes from both sides being in accord can you be sure that your decision is right; only then are you fully functioning.

Of course, there are many times when your right brain *will* make decisions alone; like a protective mother, it seems to shield the left brain from a lot of nonsense that it shouldn't be wasting its time on. For, very often, a problem isn't worth all that much time or energy, and the instantaneous solution of the right brain can—and should—dispose neatly of the matter. Or sometimes, as in an exam, you don't have the time to logically or consciously think about all the questions; here the right brain alone can really be an effective tool (which I'll get into later). But it doesn't work in reverse; once your left brain deals with a matter, the right brain is also, and automatically, in the act; therefore, if you are consciously thinking about a problem, you should be sure that both sides of your brain agree on your decision.

Even though the brain doesn't have light switches attached to it, we seem able to a certain degree to turn on the kind of activity in which we want to participate. One particular form of research in this area, known as biofeedback communication, has also only recently gotten under way, and is based on the fact that our various types of mental behavior create particular brain-wave patterns. We know that the slowest brain-wave rhythm takes place when we are so deeply asleep we are not even dreaming. As you go up the mental activity ladder, the motor (in effect) seems to shift gears and the speed of the pattern gets faster; the waves produced while you are mentally concentrating and doing problem solving are the fastest. This would seem to explain why logical and sequential thinking is so difficult and so tiring: it just takes a lot more energy! (Anyway, that's what I tell myself whenever I get up and walk away from my desk.)

We are learning to control our minds and our bodies with various methods: yoga, transcendental meditation, and Zen are some of these disciplines; however, they are spiritual in nature. Biofeedback, on the other hand, utilizes instruments that can monitor and differentiate the various brain rhythms, or the electrical impulses sent to muscles, or skin temperature. By the use of these instruments you can learn to choose and, in effect, control to some extent the particular type of mental activity you wish to engage in. Here too the future possibilities may be limitless; at this juncture no one can do more than venture a guess. However, we can—and will—utilize and adapt some of these ideas to our needs so that you can learn to effectively turn on and use both sides of your brain in making your decisions, and do so without a backpack or room full of instruments.

As for the logical side of your brain, you actually will be ordering it to work merely by concentrating on each of the sequential steps in the process of making a decision. This, obviously, is because you will be thinking verbally and linearly, in a highly structured manner—the essence of the logical approach. Since this is a step-by-step process, automatically (and by definition) the left brain will be working. Also, throughout this book, I'll give you some tools that will help stimulate the left-brain's activity.

As for the right brain, which as you know is conceptual and unstructured, it's not turned on in the same fashion. Actually, it's *always* working, except possibly in the deepest sleep; and there are also some ways to bring this intuitive side into dominant play. It is really quite simple: when you wish to use this holistic, spatial side of the brain in particular, you merely relax your intellectual thought processes and allow yourself to become receptive to all imaginative input.

In effect, you give the right brain the necessary space to function by slowing down your rhythm. You must avoid pressuring yourself; you must be willing to say, "I give up," when an answer won't come to the logical brain. You intentionally empty your mind of whatever it is that you were concentrating on, in order to make room for the spontaneous thoughts that often seem to just pop into your head, as if from nowhere, when you are at ease.

For example, I sometimes cannot consciously remember the name of someone I'm thinking of. The harder I try, the more frustrated I become. But if I change the mental subject—that is, if I stop pushing my memory and go to another matter—the name often surprisingly appears when I return to the problem. Clearing the mind and emptying it of effort seems like an incubation period that almost sets up the process of jolting awake the recalcitrant cells when you suddenly turn back to the problem. And the same continually happens for ideas. I have the feeling that the right side comes on first, almost like a starter motor, before the left brain begins to warm up. I can sit in a room, quietly listening to music, devoid of thought. And then I think: "What about _____?" Suddenly, before I have another single conscious thought, I *know* what the answer is. Intuitively, in a flash. And you know what I'm talking about; it's happened to you, too. All we must really train ourselves to do is to recognize this right-brain product, and to give it its just due.

You must not allow this relaxation process to become forced; its essence is that you be at ease, unpressured, open-minded. You should feel no strain, no conscious effort, no attempt at direction. You merely allow the brain to go limp, like a big rag doll; *that's* when the right side seems to work best. Nor is this easy; I have seen people gritting their teeth and clenching their fists as they were literally fighting to relax. So be patient with yourself; give yourself sufficient time to learn how to tune out, and then give yourself the space to allow this mood to take over.

Paradoxically, it seems that physical activity, more than anything else, is the key to accomplishing this relaxation, to turning on the right side. Or, to be more accurate, it's the switch to turn *off* the left side. Physically doing something—anything—will do it. Walk, swim, bicycle, chop wood, water plants, draw, paint, cook, bake, clean, play ball. Maybe talk with your hands, in gestures; even scream, mutter to yourself, or pound a pillow. And do these things in short bursts, without any routine; just let the action happen.

Or change your span of attention frequently. If you have been using the left brain to think and you feel the thoughts are not coming easily, interrupt yourself to do something spatial; suddenly coming back to the problem from a physical activity can trigger the functioning of the mind. Many times while writing I will be stuck for the word, or the progression of a thought. I put the whole bloody mess out of mind and go shave, or shower—and zap! When I come back to the desk there it is. Or I get up and walk around a bit; don't you remember wishing you could do this during all those interminable tests you had to take in school? It would have helped. . . .

Sometimes I jog in place, and then slowly move over to the desk; as I look down at the page that's bothering me it's almost as if I'm shaking sense into my head as I bounce. Or perhaps you'll find it effective to go for a drive. A famous composer has said he does some of his best work while out in his car; he carries a small tape recorder with him to be able to capture the tune when it suddenly comes to him. That, by the way, is a good idea even if you're not a famous composer: how often have you awakened in the middle of the night with a "great" idea, one that was probably right-brain generated and you were sure you would remember in the morning? And how often was it forgotten? The same used to happen to me; even notepads and pencils didn't help, for they were always too much trouble. But then I got a mini-cassette recorder to keep beside my bed, and now nothing is lost. In fact, when I played it back one day I was startled to hear the same idea repeated three different times, virtually word for word. Interestingly, that also happened to be one of my better ideas!

For some, doing nothing seems to be even more effective than any physical activity: lying down—as opposed to sitting up—is a great way of generating intuitive brain activity. A hammock is magic. So is just staring into a fire, relaxing in a sauna, or soaking in a hot tub. Or simply go off into a semi-darkened room, or put on some soft, relaxing music. Read something that doesn't fully capture your attention. Sometimes motion will do it: the repetitive rhythm of a train or a plane can induce a certain drowsiness and removal of mental barriers. Very effective too is a lecture, or a movie, or a television show (except for the commercials) that's not really good enough to rivet your attention yet not bad enough to arouse your anger. Or stare at a sunset, a mobile, or some tropical fish in a tank. Water of any kind—a lake, even rain—is fantastic. Whatever way you choose, just induce the trancelike state and let yourself go blank.

It's like meditation: formless and timeless, just allowing the mind to aimlessly wander and to accept all impressions from your emotions, your memories, and your experience. And we even have a word for it: daydreaming. Somehow this spatial free association allows the intellect of the left brain to pause and to breathe and—in effect—to recharge its batteries; at the same time the right brain has a chance to come alive and do its thing.

So there you are: practically a mystic. Seriously, though, just remember that the ideas, the thoughts, and the feelings that you get during this right-brain activity, and that seem to flow naturally and appear spontaneously, will be invaluable. Treasure them, and by all means heed them; put them together with the left brain so that you are using the best of both possible worlds.

Simply put, you have two very different but equally effective instruments of thought at your disposal, and you should use both of them to your advantage by having them supplement and support and constructively challenge each other, so that you—and your decisions—will profit. Neither side is better, neither side is more important; to even think this way is to flirt with disaster. Both, used together to come to your decisions, and then mutually satisfied that you are right, are indispensable to helping you think—and decide—more clearly and more wisely.

And, of course, you must realize—both sides of you—that all this knowledge, all this information, is pure gold. But it is not to be simply treasured, it is to be used. All the time. . . .

4

The Importance of
Self-Respect

What Alice went on to say, after she was interrupted by the Cat, was that she didn't much care which way she went, "so long as I get somewhere." But this forlorn cry for a goal, any goal, just to have one, is really not enough; the Cat's answer still holds. "Somewhere" is both nowhere and everywhere; it still makes no difference which way you walk. Unfortunately, such vagueness merely compounds the confusion, and it is the biggest danger we face in our need to make wise decisions. How many times have you heard others sigh—or have you yourself said—"I just can't make up my mind"? That's the clue, the warning signal; you can almost always translate it into: "I don't know what I want." This uncertainty is the basic cause of frustration, and anxiety, and un-

38

happiness; it can tear you apart. The remedy, however, is simple and all-important: you must know your pertinent goals, and you must know yourself.

That's the vital word: *yourself.* You must know what you need for your happiness and comfort, what it is that will make your life worthwhile. For, you see, if you clearly know your goals, and what you really want for yourself, making the right decisions in order to attain them becomes relatively easy. I cannot emphasize this enough: *the single most important factor in making good decisions is to know your goals.* That's the central issue: what do you want for yourself?

To many people, that's an easy question. If I asked it of you right now, in all probability your immediate reply (just as would be mine) would be, "I want to be happy." That's the obvious—and ultimate—goal for all of us. And it's a perfectly proper answer; that really *is* what we all want. But, logically and objectively, this condition is as amorphous as Alice's "somewhere," and the search for it merely leads in circles.

A woman once came to me for a divorce: it was the end of her third marriage. "It isn't a happy one," she replied to my question as to why the marriage was breaking up.

"What was wrong with the first two?" I asked.

"They weren't happy either."

I pursued it. "In what way?"

"I don't know," she said, "they just didn't work. None of them. I just wasn't happy." She broke down, crying, "And I just want to find happiness."

Unfortunately, she did not recognize the simple truth that "happiness" is only a state of mind and, because it is a condition that merely describes emotion and feeling, it has no real substance. Happiness is formless; it cannot be touched, or seen, or physically measured in any way. Nor can it be obtained or purchased; it is only to be psychologically sensed. It is within you, essentially a product of your imagination. And trying to "find" it is akin to liking pistachio ice cream: you either do or you don't. But you can't explain happiness; nor does anyone ever really understand it even though it is our ultimate goal, the state for which we all yearn. However, there are certain goals, certain values we individually have that will result in this desired condition of happiness. What these are, and how to achieve them, is the essential question that faces us.

Therefore, unlike the confused woman I've just described who was on an emotional merry-go-round that went nowhere, you must logically and intuitively analyze the matter so that you can identify the pertinent and very personal answers to this obvious question. Certainly, the nature of these values varies with each of us, for we all dance to different drummers. We are all unique, and distinct from one another, and we like and want and need different satisfactions.

Further, you must be able to translate these objectives into specific goals that are realistic and attainable, or you will always be seeking only a "somewhere." And although it sounds naive and unnecessary to say this, I would like to point out that you must know these goals in *advance* of making your decisions; recognizing them after the fact is often tantamount to regretting the choice as well. Obviously, if you don't know what you want for yourself, how can you possibly expect to make decisions that will help you to get whatever it is that you don't know you want? That's your own form of Catch 22, clearly to be avoided.

As I was doing the research for this book, I found it remarkable that every one of the people who seemed to be eminently successful (by their own standards, at least), and who consequently considered themselves extremely happy, had at the outset a clear understanding of their own personal and pertinent goals, and were then able to easily formulate a sharp delineation of them. Happiness, of course, was the motivating factor, the condition they aspired to, but all of these people had distinct and explicit ideas of what would achieve this happiness for themselves. Therefore, the first thing to ask yourself is: *what* will give you this happiness? What do you want for yourself that will make you really feel good? *That's* what you need to know.

Further, goals keep changing, and being added to. Or they should. A man I know told me that he now has great difficulty in making decisions, continually postponing his final judgment in even trivial matters. It happens that he has achieved great financial success; having decided early in life that above all else he wanted the independence that wealth would give him, he had easily achieved that goal. Because of his success, and particularly because he had always been definite and quick in his decisions, he not only is confused by his present inability in this area, but is depressed by it as well. I asked him what his present goals were and his answer was as I expected: he had none. For now, with the security of his great wealth, he is very happy. But what he hadn't realized, of course, is that this contentment is precisely why he has difficulty in making decisions now; he no longer has any pertinent and concrete goals. Because he feels he has achieved the only goal that was ever of importance to him, he no longer is asking himself: what do I want for me?

As with my wealthy friend, unawareness of one's goals is the major obstacle to making good decisions that I encounter in most of the people to whom I talk. They seem unable to say, "This is what I want for me." Too often they have not even begun to think about it, or analyze it, or define it. Or, if they have thought about their goals, they have generally done so in terms of what they *don't* want: goal setting becomes (primarily) a matter of clearing out their lives. Happiness, for them, is to be realized by getting rid of bothersome restrictions, or annoyances, or pain; in this sense their lives are at least partially suffocated. And so, for them, the attainment of a "full" life, and the happiness it represents, can best be achieved simply by getting rid of these constraints.

For one woman I know, the only goal she could think of as having any real meaning was "tranquillity." By this she really meant the freedom of being able to live her life without the compelling need of trying to totally please her husband. This was especially true in relation to his sexual desires, which he continually expected her to satisfy without any consideration for her own. She is Hispanic, and has a strong family orientation, with its preoccupation with the "woman's place" in society; consequently she feared she was depriving her husband of his traditional conjugal rights. She spent a long, arduous time ridding herself of this guilt, and is now considerably happier. But she was always entitled to this simple existence; it should not have been necessary for her to fight so hard just for what is essentially survival. However, she still has a way to go: although she now feels unfettered, she has no further positive goals.

And this is the one fault I find with almost all the various methods of today's soul-searching: they are basically negative in their approach. They are more concerned with what you should remove from your life than with what you should put into it. They focus on eliminating life's garbage rather than obtaining some nourishment that will enrich your basic existence. People who have gone through these trainings can easily tell me what they don't want in their lives, and this awareness is unquestionably of enormous value. But then many of them have great difficulty in stating what they *do* want. Their energy has been expended in merely obtaining the space to breathe; they have yet to decide how else to fill the void still remaining in their lives. They have no further goals.

At the core of not being able to know one's goals is the matter of self-respect—or, rather, the lack of it. Self-respect is one of life's great intangibles, and it means many things to many people. It may be called other names: "self-esteem" and "identity" are two that immediately come to mind. But whatever you call it, and however you seek it out, essentially it is the same thing: self-respect is the confidence of knowing your worth as a human being, coupled with a healthy concern to maintain this posture.

Self-respect is having a proper regard for yourself and what you stand for. It is having a self-image of which you're proud, and which you are determined to maintain. And it is the assurance of not only knowing your desires and your needs, but positively asserting your right to have them satisfied.

Essentially, self-respect is freedom: the independence to know, and like, and want, and expect for *yourself*. It is the liberty to laugh and to cry, to be joyful or sad, to love and to hate, to be exuberant or private. It is the right to communicate these emotions, honestly and openly, without guilt or shame, and with the expectation that you will be heard when you so bare your soul. It is the awareness of what you need to satisfy these feelings, with the courage to assume that what you are entitled to will be yours. And it is the strength to know that you will get it.

But the sum of it all is eloquently simple: self-respect is the freedom to like yourself, and want for yourself.

Obviously, this awareness of self cannot be allowed to become an infringement on the rights of others; there is a world of difference between being self-sufficient and selfish. Knowing your worth, and maintaining it by a self-concerned focus on your own needs and desires, is a highly commendable course of behavior. To be able to take care of yourself, for your own benefit and without the need for others, is the essence of mental health, and its greatest challenge. And sharing with another, or others, and caring for them fully and completely, can be the culmination of your realization of yourself as a person. Dependence on the loved ones in your life, and your corresponding responsibility to them, is not encroachment by either side; the mature demands made in a mutually sharing relationship should be fully expected and willingly fulfilled.

Only when you begin to take or demand from others that which is theirs does a relationship degenerate into selfishness. Oscar Wilde put it well: "Selfishness is not living as one wishes to live, it is asking others to live as one wishes to live." No one is entitled to encroach upon the rights of others or take undue advantage of them; that is selfish. But there are many who do (whether consciously or not), and so you had better look out for yourself. To do so is to maintain your own self-respect; you are not being selfish in turn. The two are not the same, although very often manipulative people attempt to treat them as if they are.

When my overworked friend told her lecherous husband that she was tired of constantly doing his bidding, and was putting an end to it because it really did not suit her needs any longer, he was appalled at her "selfishness" in depriving him of what (to him) were his God-given rights. He could not accept the fact that she simply wanted her own freedom, but considered her action a threat to—and deprivation of—his manliness. To him, her attempt at self-assertion was an overt and unforgivable act of selfishness. But obviously this woman was not taking something from him that was his (which of course would have been selfish); she was merely trying to make herself whole by putting herself first for once. She was only regaining her self-respect.

I have a client like this woman's husband—or, rather, I *had* such a client; there was no choice but to get him out of my life. This man is a genuine workaholic; hundred-hour weeks are barely par for him. He has enormous energy and tremendous drive, and he is so self-centered about his needs that he finds it impossible to understand that other people may have their own, somewhat different and possibly conflicting, needs. A dozen calls a day from him were usual; so were packets of mail and meetings galore. Since he is very important and active in his field, I at first enjoyed this attention and dependence on me; of course I was flattered by it. Because of this, I made a bad decision: I gave up more and more of my time to him and allowed other needs of mine—like writing this book—to suffer. And for a while he even observed some amenities, like not disturbing me while I was on vacation, or on my weekends in the country, or past midnight, unless he felt he had an emergency that absolutely could not wait until the next morning. But then *his* definition of such emergencies began to bend, and stretch; my life, which was already distended, was becoming more and more encroached upon and suffocated. I was beginning to feel sheer anger and resentment when my phone rang. And since I did not want to waste my emotional energies in this way, nor could he understand or respect my needs, I finally had to correct my earlier mistake and put him out of my life. Unfortunately, since we were also friends, he was very hurt; to this day he still takes my action as a personal rejection and cannot accept that I was merely trying to protect myself.

We're too easily vulnerable to some of our friends, and they can unwittingly take advantage of it. Friendship, for them, is a one-way street; nor do they recognize the falsity of their approach even when it is pointed out. Therefore, we simply must decide to shelter ourselves, even at the cost of losing the friend. Unfortunately, my client could not conceive of anyone else's needs or feelings, and so when I pointed mine out to him simply in an attempt at self-preservation, he instead took it as an attack upon himself. My motives were misunderstood, and assailed; I was "inconsiderate" and "selfish." But in the end my decision was simple; it had become my life or his. And then, of course, there was no contest.

With self-respect, you've got it made; without it, you're as good as dead. Without the protection of the vital element of knowing and respecting *yourself*, lack of self-esteem, like a cancer, will grow and spread, eventually suffocating your body and killing your mind. It's the root cause of the evils of the world, and we're all vulnerable to it. You must—it is vital—be willing and able to say, "This is what I want, and what I am worth. *And I will have it.*"

Therefore, if this chapter has touched you in any way, if you find yourself relating to it and thinking it has some special meaning to you, you might want to examine the question of self-respect in greater depth. Above all, be honest with yourself; don't avoid the issue. Self-deception hurts no one else quite as much as it demolishes you; the old saying "To thine own self be true" applies here better than anywhere else. Lack of sufficient self-respect easily could be the major cause of any difficulty you may have in making wise and healthy decisions.

Think about it. It makes sense.

5

Obstacles in Determining Your Goals

Lack of self-respect manifests itself and adversely affects the decision-making process in a number of ways, and I'd like to talk about some of the more common of these obstacles. They are all direct results of this deficiency, and since we constantly encounter them in trying to make our way in the world, being aware of them may help you to avoid them. The important thing is to understand these dangers clearly, and then to examine your own method of making decisions and your abilities in doing so as objectively as possible. Then, if there is any suggestion of these problems present in your own life, you can readily recognize them and effectively deal with them. Self-knowledge is the first and most important step to self-respect.

Probably the most blatant and common (as well as major) difficulty for all of us to overcome is our training. We have been programmed to not think for ourselves. Our parents were our gods, their omniscience and wisdom were beyond question, their authority was absolute. From birth we were conditioned to look for their approval and praise, and to habitually perform for this reward. Further, we were taught to not question, but to accept and emulate; "Be a good boy and do as you're told" is one of the most debilitating of parental remarks. It's a form of barter: our freedom to be ourselves for their love or—at least—approval. And if you're female in our chauvinistic society, you're really destroyed: the stigma of not being a "good girl" is even worse. Our fear of disapproval, of not being loved and, possibly, even being rejected, is one of the most powerful weapons in the arsenal of conformity; our parents unintentionally established this pattern of dread, and we then were virtually bound to live forever with the resulting insecurities and guilts.

We learned our obligations well: "I should" and "I ought" have become ingrained in our speech and in our minds. We have learned what we are supposed to do and we almost invariably do it, usually unwittingly. But even though these phrases are strongly suggestive, they are not nearly as compulsive or barbaric as "I must," which is just as prevalent. The person who believes that he "should" or "ought" or—poor soul!—"must" do this or that is a product of this malaise and can have but little real self-respect. But he does have tremendous guilt if he doesn't do what he is supposed to do; in fact, guilt is one of the most potent of the manipulative devices to which we are conditioned.

Conditioning is just as strong in regard to our goals. Invariably, they have always been determined for us by others, or set for us by society. "If you do this, then I will give you . . ." is the killer. Our parents (reflecting their own programming) indoctrinated us with what they benevolently believed we should want out of our lives. We were "guided" in our selection of schools, careers, even our husbands and wives. This usurpation of our thought processes was continued by our teachers, and compounded by our employers, our ministers, and even our friends: we have been spoon-fed all our lives. And so we never learned to think; we never learned to set our own goals; we never learned to take responsibility for ourselves. We merely learned to conform, to be what others thought we should be.

Women in particular are subject to this psychological rape. They have been taught from infancy that they are the weaker sex, obviously inferior, the ones to be taken care of. That's what men are primarily for: support, leadership, even dominance. A woman's place, with luck, is in the home, after her traditional goal of getting married, preferably to a professional man, has been achieved. If you're a woman, it's hard to escape. You're bombarded with this tripe all through your life: the schools schedule you for home economics and sewing, not shop or manual training; the ads assure you that if you use the right toothpaste and deodorants (mouth, underarm and vaginal), you are destined to capture the Lochinvar of your choice. And the implication is that you will, courtesy of Bristol-Myers and Winston-Salem, live happily ever after (provided, and only for as long as, you remain devoted to their products!). Movies, television, magazines and novels all reinforce this image of helpless femininity.

But this picture of genteel grace really represents subjugation to male authority. The medieval customs of walking on the inside of the street (to protect against being splashed by galloping horses) or having doors opened for you (after all, you *are* the weaker sex) give chivalric substance to the idiotic notion that a woman can't be trusted to take care of herself, much less be allowed to go out alone. And in return for this obedience, and the seductive fluttering of your eyelashes, men, the stronger sex, will love, honor, and support you. And they'll also treat you like a lady: they'll light your cigarettes, help you cross streets, even give you your orgasms. Only just remember, babe, who's boss. And obey.

Those, supposedly, are your goals.

The problem here is twofold: it's not only your training, if you're a woman, but the man's training as well to believe that all this garbage is true. Not only do you have to fight to break your own mold, but you also have to battle like hell to get past the stereotype of you that we men were implanted with! It's double trouble, this double standard, and you have my sympathy and support. It's a source of constant wonderment to me that you manage to free yourselves as often—fortunately—as I now find it being done among my friends. And I know I'm angry about this: I resent the years I've spent trying to take care of one woman or another, simply because both she and I were programmed to it. It's enough responsibility to take care of myself, and I'm glad I no longer have to carry that excess baggage. It's fine to care and share; it's another thing to act "Big Daddy."

Unfortunately, there are people who like to play this game in their need for an authority figure. I know several women who have become involved with men considerably older than themselves; these elders seem to represent parental figures to the younger mate, and their relationships reflect these roles. There's a sad sense of déjà vu if you close your eyes and just listen to the conversations these women maintain with their men: the evident feeling of dependence is reminiscent of childhood. There is, very clearly, an authority figure who is psychologically dominating the relationship so that the emotion is not of love between equals but rather as between parent and child. The willing acceptance of being told what to do, or want, by a respected senior is the duplicate of the pattern originally ingrained in the child, and repeats that authoritarian programming. A benevolent despot still both controls and is responsible for the child.

A man I know is in this pattern: he is somewhat past middle age, but he is unwilling to recognize or accept this. In his senile attempt to recapture his youth, he constantly seeks out girls in their twenties. He plies them with lavishments: a day at Gucci, a weekend in Palm Beach, expensive jewelry. And they, poor fools, are caught by their past. It's not so much the money he spends on them; that's only part of his attraction. More important for them is that he strikes a good figure; he could pose for any advertising agency in the stereotype of the benign father. That's the real hold he has on these women. They now have, probably more so than they ever did in their childhood, a paternal idol who will care for them, who will pay attention to them, who will tell them what to do. And so, while seriously playing at this game of house, they exploit each other: he to satisfy his own sick needs, and she because she was programmed that way. But now, with the child actually grown to adulthood (at least physically), it's even more sad, for much of the joy of self-accomplishment, especially of one's true wants, is missing at a point in life where it is even more important than it was earlier.

And so this problem of overly respecting authority is a double-edged sword. If you (male or female) are in this pattern, you are not only unable to establish your own goals because you have become accustomed to having them determined for you, but also you generally tend to accept them unquestioningly when they are set for you. The "be a good boy" line carries with it the implied threat that if you are not, you will suffer the consequences and be punished accordingly. Or, at least, carry the guilt. Therefore: do as you're told, and be rewarded. And so for the pat on the head we sell ourselves out: we eagerly become what we are expected to be. The goals, and their sequential decisions, easily become routine, then ritual; all part of the pattern. Consequently, the end product (us) is too often the last of a long line of self-reflecting mirrors, the kind where you can look into one and see hundreds of images going off into the distance. But, unfortunately, the image is always the *same*, and it's progressively getting smaller and smaller. And duller.

The regrettable, predictable result is that we have become addicted not only to accept but even to seek out an authority figure: a person to tell us what to think and do. It's not just the woman looking to replace her father; all of us do it constantly if we are not aware—and careful. For example, a friend of mine who smokes several packs of cigarettes a day once said to me, "You're lucky you don't smoke." I was surprised at the remark, for it hadn't been luck but a conscious determination on my part that led to my stopping the habit. I said this to him, and his question was revealing: "But didn't your doctor tell you to give it up?" That's my point: he knew that he too wanted to give up smoking; his use of the word "lucky" had given this away. But he needed a doctor—an authority figure—to set this goal for him and actually order him to stop. He lacked the self-respect and the self-confidence to do it for himself, nor was he willing to accept the possibility that I could stop smoking without an external command; he was crushed when he learned that I *did* do so on my own. And so he continues smoking, feeling sorry for himself and his lack of luck.

A friend of mine once dated a woman who also had this problem of needing an authority figure. She was a lovely person, but was not sufficiently respectful of her body to take care of it. Although she was overweight, the most strenuous exercise she ever performed was to brush her teeth. She professed to be aware of the aesthetic and physical consequence of this behavior, but she did nothing about correcting any of these habits. Rather, she kept hinting broadly that, given the right inducement by him, she would consider remedying these patterns. In effect, she wanted him to accept this responsibility, for she lacked sufficient self-respect to take care of herself. She too required a surrogate parent to establish her goals and program her life.

Still another aspect of authority domination is—strange as it may seem—peer pressure. It is paradoxical, but true: our friends probably do as much to make us now conform to the norm as our parents did in the beginning. In effect, the group becomes an authority "figure," one whose power is enormous. Our peers are likely to be responsible for having started us on smoking and drinking, on sex and on drugs. A lot of pre-teenage kids in our society today are smoking, for example, not only because of the macho advertisements to do so that constantly bombard them, but also because many or most of their friends are doing so. To buck their crowd is too iconoclastic, and therefore too difficult to make it worth the effort (even if they want to). They are not willing to be laughed at or ridiculed or snubbed. I know of one adolescent girl in particular who was very much into the health scene; she knew what happened to her body as a result of smoking, and she had vowed never to abuse herself in that fashion. But her "friends" got to her; she now pathetically tries to convince herself—and us—that her earlier beliefs were not valid and that she has made a conscious choice to pay the price for pleasure and is really enjoying her pack a day. Unfortunately, as it was for her, it is the same for many: it is easier to accept the weed. Incidentally, the ads themselves are also a form of authority pressure: they are merely trading in on the training we as parents supply. Having brainwashed our children into believing that it is expected of boys to be virile "he-men" and for girls to be beautiful and desired by these heroic male figures, we then cannot blame the advertising agencies that subtly suggest these glories as direct consequences of smoking; or whatever else they may be selling.

As we grow older, the peer pressures continue: goals are set, usually implicitly, that we are expected to attain; interestingly, however, they are not to be exceeded. Aggressiveness and ambition are admired, but only in the abstract. It's okay if it happens to someone you once knew, and he has made it; if you show the same signs, however, you're sure to be considered "pushy," even gross. In essence you're supposed to remain a conforming part of the group. You may want a better car than your neighbor, but the basic goal (the car) is virtually the same for all. This can also be said for the house (in suburbia), for our clothes, our vacations, and the like. And so it is with most of the life style: it is usually unimaginative and generally determined by what the group wants.

This pressure holds true on the job as well: don't do more than your peers do, or you will upset the system. And if you try too hard, ostracism is your reward; nobody (they will let you know) likes a smart-ass. You are continually expected to conform, to accept as your goals the goals of the many. And so you learn how not to set your own. Or you're forced by your peers to conform. For example, in colonial America adults were expected to marry for the good of society; life was made very uncomfortable for one who wished to live alone. In Connecticut, which is typical, a gentleman with such an antisocial desire in the 1630s was taxed 20 shillings a week for the "selfish luxury of solitary living," and a woman who was still unmarried at the advanced age of twenty-five was scorned as a "dismal spectacle." Maybe we're not so bad off after all.

All this dependence on, and searching for, authority figures to guide and lead us is part of the programming we learned early in life, and is often directly linked to another pattern I described earlier: the habit, and inertia, of continuing a decision made at some point in the past. Having embraced a goal set by our parents or our peers, and having thereafter fallen into the convenient and comfortable habit of believing in its sanctity, we find it very difficult to subsequently question its validity.

The two patterns compound and reinforce each other synergistically, to our detriment. We accept the "shoulds" and the "oughts," and we stop thinking. For it is easier, on many levels, to regard almost as gospel the goals already established and the decisions already made; and it is certainly safer in terms of the response of the society in which we live. The assumptions become "fact," virtually chiseled in stone. And the defense mechanisms paralyze the brain and further the debilitation; the present state of affairs is rarely if ever examined, and new goals are even less frequently set. We easily become part of the culture, such as it is, and then we are lost. I'll go into this later on, with some ways of recognizing this trap and dealing with it.

Another major trap to beware of is the fear of failure. The natural tendency to avoid this regrettable result can often lead to total paralysis. It's perfectly understandable, for none of us wants to fail at anything we do. Normally, merely setting a goal generates a certain excitement; the stimulation this creates is part of the joy of the attempt to achieve. This thrill, of course, is to be welcomed and is healthy. The element of risk, possibly danger, that is inherent in every attempt to attain a goal is part of its fun and an important element in keeping us alert and aware, and cautious and careful. But although the achievement of our goals brings great satisfaction, and success in anything we undertake is much to be desired, we are sometimes reluctant to make the attempt because of our corresponding fear of failure.

This fear of failing too often begins with our parents; as I pointed out earlier, they set their goals for us. Maybe if they considered themselves successful, they wanted us to emulate them, or possibly they wanted us to be better than they were, and to have the advantages they never did. So, generally, we were "guided" either to repeat their lives or to attain goals that they hadn't been able to achieve, but we were expected to easily accomplish. We were led to believe that we would disgrace them if we didn't succeed, and that the resultant embarrassment and shame was the equivalent of a national catastrophe. And the suggestion was that if we were to fail, it was because we didn't love them enough. ("If you really care for Mommy, you'll make her proud of you by doing well in school. . . .") The pressures on us as children were enormous; and our resentments, conscious or unconscious, just as great. And, of course, either because of the rebellion within, or because the goals actually were not so easy, or even because we didn't really care about goals that were not our own to begin with, we failed frequently.

I know two men who had the goal of being doctors set for them by their parents. One is the son of a doctor, and the other the son of a man who had wanted to be a doctor but was unable to afford medical school. Neither of these two men achieved this parental goal, and both now consider themselves—understandably but unrealistically—abject failures. Both are, emotionally, the products of their would-be proud parents.

This fear of failure may also be due to the converse: many children grow up indoctrinated with the nightmare that they *are* dismal disappointments. They have been badgered and bullied into believing they can't do anything; invariably a parent has resignedly told them how it can be done better, or criticized the child for not having known how to do it in the first place. The self-doubts and insecurities are started early with all the lecturing advice: "Do this" or, more frequently, the negative command implying you're a fool: "Don't *do* that!" Or worse: "Won't you ever learn?" And so any confidence is destroyed early by this demeaning self-image and the inability to develop—and engender—any responsibility. The failures go hand in hand with this lack of self-esteem.

A teen-ager I know, the product of a broken marriage, is being destroyed in just this way. Her father, in an attempt to teach her responsibility, gives her a weekly allowance so that she can learn how to take charge of her own finances. But her mother has unintentionally sabotaged the intent: she "knows" that her daughter is too young—and, by implication, too dumb—to be trusted with this small munificence. Therefore, this would-be do-gooder commandeers the money when it arrives, promising to save it for her daughter's later welfare. Unfortunately, the mental health of the child is being damaged in the process; she's learning that she can't be trusted to take care of herself.

Here too the child's own society does it as well: kids love to put down others of their ilk, and oftentimes cruelly at that. Possibly, in some way, they are trying to regain some small feeling of security for themselves. Possibly they're only trying to get even with a world with which they really can't cope. They make up nicknames that hurt; they form their own small, exclusive cliques; they taunt each other; and they gloat over another's mishaps. Their media, too, enhance the self-doubt. In many comic books they pick up, on many television shows they watch, they are bombarded with their faults: pimples, weight, bad breath, body odor, tangled hair, yellow teeth, total disaster. What a self-image! No wonder these kids feel secondhand, abject failures at the grown-ups' game of life.

Either way: having fulfilled the dire predictions by failing, or having been unable to achieve the unrealistic goals that were established for him, the child is understandably more tentative in his next attempts. And as he grows older, this hesitancy is compounded by the occasional failures that are normally part of everyone's life and are to be expected. But the pressures to succeed are so intense, and the seeming disappointment of others at the child's lack of success so great, that he develops an understandable resistance against trying again. This terror of failing can sometimes loom so large that it becomes overpowering and even paranoid; it petrifies and paralyzes, and finally results in total inaction. To the person so burdened, the specter of this disgrace is such a frightening prospect that it is easier to take the coward's way out: just avoid the whole pattern. The rationalization is simple: "If I set a goal, I may fail. Therefore, I won't set a goal, so there is no chance of failure." It's sure and it's safe.

The net result is that this person is eminently "successful"; he has achieved everything he wants by the simple expedient of not wanting very much. In effect, it's a reverse self-fulfilling prophecy. And it's completely self-defeating. I am reminded of a woman I know who was asked by her therapist what her income goal was for the coming year. When she gave the figure, he was saddened but not surprised; it was considerably less than they both knew she was capable of earning. But, of course, that's why she was with him: to try to regain her self-respect.

Sometimes this fear of failure is based on the experiences of others, although the effect is the same. I know a fellow who was best man at the weddings of three of his friends, all of whom subsequently divorced. He boasts that he will never be a fool like them; failure, he says, is not his bag. But he's more lonely than they are; in fact they're still trying, now on their second attempts. He's still home alone.

There is no joy to be found in this Mudville of passivity and negativism; only stagnation and the barrenness of boredom. Living in such a vacuum because it is seemingly safe is no fun. Taking chances in life not only keeps it from becoming monotonous, but may also save you from becoming a vegetable.

Most importantly, you must recognize that "failure" is only what you think it is; you're not a failure unless you consider yourself one. No one else can make you a failure; you are the only person who has that power. (And the outside world is often far more generous than we are in our self-evaluation: most critics are nowhere near as hard as we are on ourselves.) Further, failure is an absolute term, implying totality; therefore it is not a real state of being unless and until you stop setting goals for yourself, and stop trying to attain them. That's failure: to quit, and to withdraw from life. But as long as you keep trying, you can never be a failure. You may not achieve a particular goal from time to time; we all have these moments. But you are not a failure because of it.

A woman I know was afraid to take the test for a driver's license, for she knew she was going to fail it. She kept delaying with one excuse or another, until finally the friends who had been chauffering her around on their weekends at the beach insisted that she postpone no longer. Of course she flunked, which was sufficient confirmation for her of all her dire predictions. However, her friends refused to accept this; their goal was clear. So she (unwillingly) took the test again, and not unexpectedly she failed it again. But by the third try, when she realized that she was not being allowed the luxury of remaining a failure, she decided to buckle down to the test and stop wasting her time. And so—you guessed!—she passed. Maybe she's not one of the best drivers around, but at least she's mobile. Had she stopped after her first or second try, and accepted the "failure," she would now be sitting home alone. But by not quitting or, rather, not being allowed to quit, she eventually achieved success.

Even apparently successful people, by whatever standards this is judged, have moments when they feel as if they are abject failures. Is the multimillionaire I described who has been unable to have—or to buy—a continuing, long-term, and happy relationship with any of the numerous women of his choice a "success" or a "failure"? Isn't he both, at the same time? Obviously it depends on your point of view and how you set the standards. If money is your goal, he's very successful; if a relationship is your criterion, he's not.

Even in one's chosen field of endeavor you cannot achieve success all the time. In fact, people who are successful at certain things also can be suffering from and be hindered by this fear of failure. The success itself sometimes causes the terror, for it means that more will then be expected of you in the future which, therefore, increases the possibility that you may fail. I wrote a fairly successful book on backgammon some time ago, and thereafter found it difficult to enjoy the game—or even play it well. Because I was the authority, everyone wanted to beat me; and whenever someone did, it was with great glee at my apparent "failure." The pressure on me not to lose was enormous, far more so than before I wrote the book. And so I simply stopped playing for a while; by this avoidance I was precluding the possibility of a blow to my ego. But what I really gave up was the fun of participation—which is no fun at all.

You must simply realize that you're human and, as such, you will be successful in some things you attempt and not successful in others. We all succeed at times; and we all, either because of our own mistakes or because of factors we do not control, don't succeed at other times. And you cannot allow yourself to fear the lack of success to such a degree that you refuse to even try to achieve it. Not to be willing to take a chance on improving your life by refusing to set goals for yourself is tantamount to refusing to get up in the morning and face the day. Either way, it's a form of living death, an acceptance of failure as a final, complete, total state of being. And without even trying. One of my dearest friends has a Victorian charm on her key-chain that succinctly says it all: "Little risk, little reward." And it's just as true today as it was then, and as it always will be.

So remember this: for whatever number of goals you set, some will be achieved and some will not. The important thing to do is to set them, and then constantly try to improve the ratio of those that are attained to those that are not. Forget the word "failure"; let posterity worry about it (should it care). Don't let this preoccupation bog you down in measurements, or labels, or fears. Set your goals, try your damndest to attain them, and don't be panicked if you don't achieve them all. No one can, or does. But you must keep trying. And for those goals you do achieve—you're a success!

The other side of this coin is psychologically more complex: there are some people who are afraid of success. For a variety of reasons, these individuals feel guilty if they achieve something nice for themselves, or prove themselves to be better than another, and this guilt can be very painful. Therefore, they will go to great lengths to avoid such feelings by not allowing the simplest desire to enter their thoughts. This behavior is based on the neurotic belief that you are selfish if you make demands for yourself, and of course you will not be loved if you are selfish. So the resultant precaution is that you should not specify any goals, for if you do, you just might attain them. It's easy, and it's safe; no goals means no chance of pain. But Oscar Wilde's comment on this is all too true: "Self-denial is simply a method by which man arrests his progress."

A woman I know does this very well; she has managed to convert every potential relationship into—at most—a friendship. Platonic, that is. She is unable to accept the fact that she does want a man in her life to share with, and live with, and love with; this is more than she is entitled to. And so she doesn't allow it to happen. Ever.

This self-denial also sets up tremendous conflicts for many people when they go out into the world. Our society ostensibly approves of competitiveness and even aggressiveness; you're supposed to be successful. Yet should these masochistic souls be unfortunate enough (by their convoluted standards) to achieve some small measure of recognition, they go to inordinate lengths to deny their responsibility for having accomplished this. The word "lucky" is the apology you hear. "I was lucky to get the job"; "I was lucky to get the promotion"; "I was lucky . . ." about everything! There is no room in their psychology for a simple acknowledgment that they may have a brain, or even a small talent; such immodesty would be monumentally traumatic. This self-deprecation, with the resultant embarrassment if one is even slightly successful, leads to an ever-increasing and stronger denial of all goals, from the most minor to the deepest of interpersonal relationships.

This fear of asking for oneself also begins with our parents. The admonition is essentially only a slight variation on the one that was used to program us to our authority needs: "Be a good child and leave us alone." That's what you're told to do: go off and play, or read, or watch your television set (only keep the volume down). The implication is clear: if you disturb your parents by asking for something for yourself, or even if you merely wish to share your feelings with them, you are not good. Should you impose your wants on them, you are selfish for doing so, and this behavior is, obviously, bad! Of course, bad children are not loved; so, in dread of losing this reward, you learn to be "good" and stop bothering your folks by asking for yourself. The lesson is well-learned: it is wrong to ask.

Then you go out into the world, and the training is reinforced. You want to be liked, and you remember how you were loved: "Don't want, and don't ask, and in this way you will be good and we will like you forever." Even the simple communication of feelings is to be suppressed; stoicism and acceptance of your lot are treated as virtues. And so again you don't allow yourself to ask, or to want; you also learn to fear success. For, if you do succeed, it will be clear proof to the world that you *did* want. That's one of the reasons the civil service is so popular; it really has no goals.

And there you are: don't set goals, or you may attain them. One of my clients, for example, told me one day that he wanted to be rich, *very* rich, and he had a scheme that he thought would accomplish this. Then a look of guilt came over his face, and he apologized (not to me, but to the specters within him): "Well, not *too* rich—I know that's not nice." *That* goal died before birth.

The concept of self-denial has even subtler roots. Our religions preach it as a way of life, usually as the only sure pathway to the goal of the heavenly afterlife. You know the attitude: abstain today, and it's hats and horns tomorrow! You're led to believe that sacrifice strengthens you, and is good for the soul; the more you suffer, the more Godlike you are. Overgenerosity is often the facade for this self-abnegation: do for others until you drop, and only then can you hope to have done enough. In fact, it's really an inverse point system: the less you want now, the more you'll get later. At least that's the promise—or, maybe, it's only the rationalization. Another guise for this asceticism is to "understand": you should have patience with, and acceptance of, the other person's foibles. That's noble and virtuous, you're told; it's also the road on which you'll be trampled by the less self-sacrificing herd.

The logical conclusion for all these paths is self-destruction; we all know people whose actions seem almost designed to achieve the direct opposite of what they would be presumed to want for themselves. For example, I know a lovely young woman who is now in her early thirties. She is bright, and pretty, and has great intelligence; she has a very good job in a field that is noted for the quality of the people who are in it. If she allowed herself the luxury of expressing a goal, she probably would want more than anything else to have a meaningful and permanent relationship; I am sure this achievement would give her greater pleasure than any other. Her friends, who are more aware of her needs than she is, keep trying to arrange dates for her because she herself will not make any attempts to meet new people. However, all the dates they arrange end up the same way: pure disaster. The first phone call from the man, and even the first date, is usually pleasant and fun; she is bright and does have a sense of humor. But by the second date, the self-destruction has begun: she has become cranky and nasty, and succeeds in making the evening as unpleasant as possible; one that should only be forgotten. Of course, unless the man is a masochist, he's not going to see her again. Why should he? And even if he was sufficiently impressed by her positive qualities so that he's willing to accept this unpleasant experience as merely a momentary aberration and take a chance once again, he quickly gets straightened out on the next phone call to her to arrange that date. She's curt, cold, and highly unreceptive. The message is crystal clear: go away. This woman's friends have questioned her about this obvious (to them) self-destructive pattern, but she is totally unaware of her actions and their predictable results. Unfortunately, many people have this fear of wanting something for themselves. And, as I've pointed out before, this reluctance to say "this is what I want for me" is one of the foremost signs of disrespect for one's self.

There is yet another problem in stating a goal: it is the inability to be realistic. I'm thinking particularly of that segment of our society that has been brought up to believe that they are little princes or princesses on pedestals; consequently they deserve only the best and should not accept anything less. Now, it's fine to want to travel first-class all the way; I'm highly in favor of it. But with these poor misguided souls it is both an expectation and a demand. They are "entitled" to, and must have, perfection in all they do; anything less than that ultimate state is unworthy of them, to be avoided like the plague. In this sense there is a similarity to the fear of failure, except that here the goal is higher; if it is not total "perfection" it is, by definition, failure. A degree of achievement that would satisfy most people is of no value here. I have shopped with some of these unfortunates who have agonized over the pattern of a bath towel; I know a man who is dodging falling plaster in his living room because he's not sure of the best color he should paint his apartment. My friend who couldn't pick a tie had at least half a dozen that were great combinations with his suit of the day; he was simply terrified that the one he wore might not be perfect. For these unfortunates and the others like them, nothing is ever quite right, nor will it ever be as long as they continue with their delusion.

The simple truth is that there is no such thing as perfection; that word is yet to be anything more than an abstract concept incapable of attainment. It is as amorphous as "happiness," or "somewhere," and when allowed to enter into and affect our lives is as dangerous. Simply recognize and realize that perfection is an absolute that cannot be measured, or even be accurately defined. As a practical matter it is meaningless and therefore totally unrealistic; any use of this term should be rejected as a false guide. I know several bachelors (male and female) who have this problem; the need for perfection in the mate keeps them living solitary lives, continually seeking, constantly lonely. For them, because of this fear of not making the perfect choice (not to mention the impossibility of doing so), they are forced to not make any. It's easier to say, "I am looking," or, "I'm thinking about it." That's really not a lie, and it suggests great intelligence calmly at work, a dignified posture much to be desired. But what this really translates to is the inability to face reality, to recognize that life is not perfect and that frailty is human. These people are, in fact, actually living in a fantasy.

This need for perfection is often compounded by the dread of the permanence that I talked about earlier. There is nothing worse than the combination of the terror of being trapped in a choice that is not only less than perfect but must also be borne for life. The marriage vow "till death do us part" is probably the most frightening example of this; it seems to leave absolutely no room for mistake or change. So, because of the need to find perfection in a mate, and the realization that the commitment to marriage should be one of the major and more permanent of the decisions in one's life, many people avoid the relationship simply because it may be less than perfect. They are unwilling, or unable, to balance and weigh and evaluate realistically; if they gave up this fantasy of perfection they might have a very happy relationship. But the fear that they might get into a situation that is long-range, and not quite perfect, leads to an avoidance of any meaningful commitment and results in the solitude of continually seeking.

These, then, are the major reasons why goals are avoided, or badly established. We look for an authority to set them for us, or we habitually accept those that are—or have been—given to us by others. Or we're afraid of failure, or programmed to it; so it's easier—and safer—not to try. Maybe we feel the guilt of wanting, or we seek perfection and therefore are unable to be realistic about what we should want. But whatever the cause, if you are not thinking of your goals and establishing them for yourself, you are only vegetating; you're merely maintaining an existence. Which, of course, is not life, and makes absolutely no sense.

To live life you need only one rule, there is only this one absolute: you must, at all times, have *yourself* in mind. You have to be aware of what you want for your happiness, what will make your life worthwhile. You have to know, and believe, that you are entitled to your fair share of the earth's rewards, and you have to be prepared to insist on your right to them. You have to recognize and respect your own worth as a human being, and you have to be ready at all times to assert and maintain this worth. In short, you have to be self-respectful; you cannot allow any of the problems I've been talking about to stop you. Erich Fromm said it succinctly and well: "The duty to be alive is the same as the duty to become oneself." *That's* the only way of life that makes sense.

To this end, the most important thing for you to do is to have, at all times, goals in mind. And they should be *your* goals; no one else's. It is true that they may be ephemeral and may not be those that you will live with forever, and it is certain that they are not absolutes in the sense of perfection. But they *are* at least the guidelines of the present. It is clear that the need for your own goals is the one permissible permanence, even if the goals themselves vary and change from time to time; they must always be present in order to serve as the homing beacon. Without them, you are lost, floundering, despondent, and frustrated. With them you are alive, vital, and totally in command of yourself and your destination. For that's what goals are: places to go. Or rather, places that you want to go to.

6

Determining Your Goals

My daughter Sara and I recently drove across the country to Arizona; we were visiting my sister in Phoenix, roughly 2500 miles from New York. In planning this drive, we scheduled six days to do it; not exactly a leisurely jaunt, but not a hard push either. As it turned out, this was a fun trip, and we would gladly do it again anytime.

In a very simplistic sense, this trip to Phoenix is analogous to our life goals. For that's what *they* are: destinations, places to go, things to accomplish. In essence, goals are what you want for yourself; they represent the achievements that will make you happy. And knowing what they are can give you the strength and the power to think clearly, and consequently to determine and control the nature and course of your own destiny. Goals are the signposts and milestones of your life; they give it substance and meaning. They provide perspective and dimension throughout your day, every day; and it is they that must in the final analysis guide, shape, and determine your decisions and your ultimate course of action. Further, goals are the standards against which your actions and accomplishments are evaluated and measured. Properly thought out, they can make your life easier, fuller, and more fun. If they are not thought out, life can be hell.

And, when your goals *are* achieved, you derive a tremendous feeling of accomplishment and satisfaction that is quite unlike anything else. But too few people really—and clearly—know their overall goals, and this lack of self-knowledge is the one factor more than any other that results in bad decisions. That's why I emphasize this matter of goals; you should too.

You realize, of course, that Phoenix was not really meaningful in and of itself; it was only the place we had to get to if we were to achieve our actual goal—the reaffirmation of our family ties. Essentially, this is what we wanted; this was our purpose, our long-range goal. Consequently, the physical means of getting there and the steps involved were not important in themselves, just so long as they helped us achieve our ultimate objective. We could have flown to Phoenix, or taken a bus or a train; it mattered not in terms of this goal. If we had met my sister and her family in Denver, say, or if they had come to New York to visit us instead, this too would not have changed the desired end result; it merely would have changed the *place* in which it could happen. All that differed was the specific location where the reunion would take place; the purpose of the meeting, being qualitative, was always the same and did not depend in any way on the specific incidents of place, or method of arriving there, or the steps in doing so.

Further, once the family did get together, there was no tangible way to evaluate the result. Each of us in our own individuality would feel a sense of satisfaction, or not; and each of us would feel it to a greater or lesser degree than would the others. Nor was there ever a specific moment at which we would know that the family ties were once again whole; this was a subjective feeling that differed for each of us.

That's precisely what our long-range goals are; they are matters of value, qualitative and not quantitative, incapable of being precisely measured or determined. They are right-brain feelings—amorphous, intuitive, emotional, even surreal. By definition (mine), they do not have parameters or boundaries or size; they have only a psychological presence. For example: I wanted a house in the country that had a feeling of space and also a good deal of privacy. Neither quality can be measured, nor should there be an attempt to do so; however, I can tell you that when I found the house I now own, I *knew* that it was right and that it had sufficient of these necessities to suit me. But knowing clearly *before* I bought what feelings I wanted satisfied has given me immense pleasure and will continue to do so for a long time to come. Similarly, you should bear in mind that long-range goals are not containers waiting to be filled and holding just so much; they are really broad objectives or, more accurately, overall and pervading directions and guides that help shape and give value and meaning to your life.

Having measurable dimensions is one of the attributes of short-range goals; they are concrete and specific, and so clearly defined that there is no question as to whether or not we achieve them. They are simple statements of quantitative need: a particular thing must be obtained, or done. There is nothing abstract about them, as there is with the long-range qualitative goals. Take money, for example, a very important factor in our society. I think it is obvious that a desire for a certain amount of money (to buy a new car, say) is really a short-range objective, whereas the long-range goal in one's life is not for an exact sum but rather for the emotional feeling that flows from the concept of wealth (as with my millionaire friend who wanted the "independence" money would give him).

I'll put it differently: although we may feel that certain specific, tangible things may be necessary to attain as immediate goals, and we may even refuse to settle for less, many *different* material things can each in its own way help us to satisfy a qualitative long-range goal. For example, a person may attain a sense of achievement by any one of a multitude of specific accomplishments; the thing that does it for one individual may be quite different from that of another person. It may be based on the size of his house, or his bank account, or even his car; it may be a job title or some artistic endeavor like performing in a community play. Whichever, these are only instruments in the attainment of this long-range goal that represents success; in turn, it is this amorphous feeling of achievement that creates the ultimate happiness. And this qualitative sense of satisfaction is the same for each of these people; the tools that achieved this, however—the short-range goals—can and do vary widely.

Short-range goals, being tangible, are also only ephemeral; once they are accomplished, the satisfaction is usually both immediate and short-lived. How often have you been wild with desire to meet someone in particular; when you finally did, how long did that ecstasy last? And the bank account is never large enough; the car was probably outgrown by the time it needed its first waxing; and the house will always have to get bigger and, sooner or later, "need" a pool, which then will "have" to be heated. However, the emotional desire for the roots and security that a "home" (of whatever size) represents supercedes the specifics: this qualitative goal is ongoing and therefore controlling. And that's exactly what I mean: the short-range tangible goals, and the happiness they bring, keep changing; the long-range ones just keep going on, and the satisfaction they give is much more lasting.

A note of caution: please do not get bogged down in words, or definitions, or artificial time boundaries. A "short-range" goal is exactly what you mean by it. I'm not a prophet on the mount who can easily pontificate and arbitrarily set time limits, as some of the books attempt to do; it is patently ridiculous to make statements like "short-range goals take place within a month at most," and long-range goals are only those that are "more than several years" away. I believe there is no specific or fixed time span for any of these that can have a universal meaning: there are no magic numbers. And that's why I like the distinction between "qualitative" and "quantitative," which I think is valid for all.

However, if you want to use deadlines, or dates, or time periods, by all means do so. It may help you to set goals for yourself that you want to accomplish in one year, or one month, or whatever. Or you may prefer to set a schedule of stages you wish to accomplish by certain times in order to be aware of your progress toward the larger goal. However you do it, remember that these words and phrases and temporal segments are all only tools; they are for your use only, and for your benefit.

My point is that you must choose and use those methods that are of value to you; no one can determine a time frame for you. Each person, and each situation, varies. The man who has the goal to attain success, which for him is represented by his becoming president of his company, may have to spend many years to accomplish this; the same feeling of personal satisfaction may be achieved in a few months by the football player who wins the Super Bowl game. The temporal difference is meaningless. All that is important is that you recognize the difference between those goals that are qualitative and those that are merely quantitative; I believe that this delineation is the only meaningful one. By understanding and using this distinction it will be easier for you to make better decisions—all the time.

The reason, it seems, is clear: long-range goals, when achieved, are the ones that result in a general feeling of overall happiness and satisfaction; the short-range ones are short-lived as well. It's fine to have both and, in fact, I believe this to be preferable; nothing could be better than achieving your overall desires while deriving great pleasure along the way. For it very often happens that short-range goals are merely steppingstones to larger short-range goals—intermediate ones, if you wish. These intermediates can also relate to each other in varying degrees and build on themselves in a continuous sequence, so that you finally and almost effortlessly attain your desired end of the overall, qualitative goal.

On a very unsophisticated level, my trip to Phoenix illustrates this well: it was a carefully planned progression of relatively minor steps so that we would arrive at our destination in the most comfortable and practical manner under the circumstances, with each step contributing to this final accomplishment. Road maps and thermos bottles filled the car, and we had several places in mind that we wanted to visit for typical tourist-type sight-seeing. The drive was divided into fairly equal daily segments, and we had made our various overnight reservations in advance. These were our "intermediate" goals. And, in order to prevent the daily trip from becoming tedious, we continually set numerous short-range objectives: "38 miles more to Santa Fe" (where we were sure there was a McDonald's, Sara's favorite); "90 miles to the Painted Desert"; "we'll stop for gas pretty soon." Obviously these "goals" were all totally unimportant in themselves; they could be changed or altered virtually at will, since none of them had any particular or substantial overall effect on our ultimate destination of Phoenix. After all, one brand of gasoline is pretty much the same as the rest; they all power the car with no perceptible difference. Nor can I tell—or care—if it's a Big Mac or a Whopper. And, if we skipped or added a sight to see, it was also no big deal; we were loose in that regard as well.

But the point is that we set certain daily goals for ourselves, even if they were relatively inconsequential and continually changing; by attaining these in easy stages we could more easily and comfortably reach our nightly objectives of a place to rest. Similarly, each of these relatively mid-range goals, even though susceptible to substitution (I can't tell a Howard Johnson room from one at a Holiday Inn either), was a necessary sequential step in the successful accomplishment of the final goal of Phoenix. Our days, and our goals, were cumulative; all were determined by, and added up to, this ultimate destination. The detours that we took, the minor changes in plan we made, were also always governed by and directed toward that one main goal. And each of these minor goals, when attained, gave us its own momentary pleasure while contributing to our overall happiness. Like Candide, we were enjoying the best of both worlds.

Of course it is obvious that, as with everything in life, quality is more important than quantity; so it is with your goals. But I do not mean to suggest that long-range goals are sacrosanct; nothing is. Although they are qualitative dimensions of your life, and require the most thought and care in their selection, they are neither final nor forever. All your goals, even these very valuable ones, are merely steppingstones or building blocks for the next one; you should remain flexible in this regard. There should *always* be another goal to strive for: yesterdays are not todays. My millionaire friend who could no longer make decisions was not able to do so because he had no real desires, no pertinent needs; and so he found himself vegetating in a plush-lined rut. However, when he finally realized this he began to use his abilities to help certain charitable groups he cared about, and now he is once again in command of himself.

This growth may also be the supplanting of a new goal for an old one; an architect I respect has said that man requires the vital stimulus of shifting light, passing times, and the changing of the seasons. As it is with the environment, so it is with your goals; each is subject to change and substitution, if and when you feel the desire or the need. It may not be easy, for a lot of dues have often been paid to get you on the way, and none of us likes to waste the time and effort; instead, however, you should consider it to be an improvement with age, like a vintage wine.

Of course, it is imperative that you are aware of this change in your goals when they occur; this knowledge can keep you from making a bad decision. For example, a man I know was in an unhappy marriage and, possibly as a result of this, began to have an affair with a woman who worked in his office. At first he thought of it as merely ego and sex gratification; then the relationship seemed to ripen, and so he decided to divorce and remarry. However, between the two events—that is, after his divorce from his first wife but before the vows to number two—he suddenly realized that he was merely substituting one relationship for another, and also that he really was enjoying the newly discovered feeling of being a free spirit. And so he stayed single; the long-range goal he had once desired, and married for, was no longer important.

So be aware of the continuing probability that you and your values will change and grow; obviously it is far better to recognize this as soon as possible when it happens and act accordingly. It makes perfectly good sense: any decision based on a discarded or obsolete goal *must* be bad. Therefore, you should constantly examine and reevaluate your thinking as clearly and as accurately as possible, so that you always know what your long-range qualitative goals really are at that moment. That's the best way to achieve happiness.

Generally you will find your important goals to be oriented in four major areas: family, career, creativity, and social needs. By "family" I mean your relationship with a husband, wife, lover. It may also include children, parents, brothers and sisters, even home; it's whatever "family" means to you, neither more nor less. "Career" generally means, to most people, their daily job; that is, their main field of economic endeavor, as opposed to a venturesome fling in a less financially rewarding direction. "Social" should cover a large territory including friends, hobbies, entertainment, and recreation. Then there is the area of achievement and recognition: the creative development that means personal growth.

Each is a separate aspect of your life, and you should recognize the fact that you probably have goals in each of these sectors. However, use these divisions as you wish; enlarge or adapt them to fit your life style. I present this breakdown as merely a tool designed only to help you better understand your own life, to know what your goals really are. It's like using an architect to plan your house; a good one doesn't design it for himself, but helps you—the client—to identify, determine, and then achieve your own values. That's what I'm trying to do here.

The question of what is of long-range importance and value to a person in any of these areas is complex, and is not commonly asked. If you already know this, that's great; usually, however, it requires a good deal of very tough soul-searching to come up with answers. It's a very personal and private thing to analyze your inner being, even if it is merely in the desire to know and not in any way a matter of self-judgment. It can be difficult, possibly painful, to bare your deeply held feelings even if only to yourself. Consequently, this self-appraisal is a matter which is rarely faced and is easily avoided. But to ask yourself, honestly and specifically, what it is that you really want from life, what it is that will give you satisfaction and pleasure, is the only sensible, logical approach to getting clarity into your life and wisdom into your decisions. Nor do you constantly have to have goals in all the areas I've mentioned; here, too, you will find that at certain times in your life one area or another will be most important; and here, too, it is only for you to say.

So let's ask the question: what are the qualitative things that you most value for yourself, that will give you the most happiness?

This is where many people generally have great difficulty. One very effective way to come up with some answers is to relax: just sit back and let your thoughts float freely. Since these are right-brain feelings we are trying to determine, let it take over for a while: meditate, daydream, induce a self-hypnosis that may help you to put aside the constrictions and possible closely held beliefs of your life. Let your mind wander; fantasize about what you have always wanted to do. Try to go back to your early past; try to remember what you once wanted. Think of what might have been if it weren't for all the pressures and compromises in your life. Start with the line "You know, once upon a time I really wanted to . . ." Then think about what you once wanted to do: what was it? *What was it?* Concentrate on empty air, or space, or an object or sound; take time to relax. Do some self-hypnosis: forget today and . . . think . . . back. . . . What did you really want to do . . . once upon a time?

Play this game of free association; where it leads may surprise you. (Or, possibly, others.) A young woman I met at a dinner party, whose reserve and tongue were somewhat loosened by a few glasses of wine, sat back in her chair and let her mind go free at my suggestion of this approach. Suddenly she sat bolt upright, startled and frightened; she reluctantly confided that she "might be" sorry that at this point in her life she was about to be married. In fact, she realized, she was most concerned that she was going to miss out on a great deal of life's experiences by not spending some time traveling abroad. She had always wanted to do so, and she had wanted to do it by herself, alone, learning about the world and the people in it, and helping make it a better place to be. Of course, she said, she did want to marry and have a home and family—but not right now.

Typically, her desire for immediate marriage was in fact the aspiration of her traditional parents, who had instilled in her the conviction that this was the normal and much-to-be-hoped-for goal of any healthy girl; consequently, she was now about to become a housewife who had forgotten—and foregone—her own personal needs. But this newfound self-awareness evidently jolted her; I have since heard that she joined the Peace Corps and is now off doing all sorts of good deeds. And, of course, she clearly was not so much in love as she was imbued with the idea that she was *supposed* to be in love. Fortunately, in this instance, the parental goals were not allowed to dominate and constrict her life; her own sense of self took over in time.

Anything that aids in arriving at some answers to this question of what are your goals is of value, and any of the right-brain turn-on devices I've talked about earlier that help you come up with these answers are worth trying. Or you might try the direct wish-fulfillment approach: if a good fairy were to suddenly appear and offer you three wishes for the rest of your life, what would they be? Or what would you do if you won a million-dollar lottery? Here's another: imagine you are going to receive a letter or a phone call or, even better, a telegram tomorrow morning: what would you most like it to say? And still one more: would you like to trade your place in life with someone else? And if so, with whom—and why? Try some of these tricks; try *anything* that will help you to recognize your goals.

Another way to do this is to stimulate left-brain activity: try to compel yourself to think logically. Most effective in accomplishing this is to take pencil in hand and put down on a piece of paper the answer to the question of what are your goals. It is a truism among professional writers (who do it for a living) that 95 percent of all artistic inspiration is the placing of the seat of the pants upon the seat of the chair; maybe you can utilize this device to come up with some brilliance of your own. It is also true that sitting upright, at a desk, is another good left-brain stimulus. Or try this: a writer client of mine does a crossword puzzle every morning to get his verbal brain working. There is evidently some merit to this: he not only makes a good living, but he has also won an Emmy for his work! Realize that forcing yourself to think logically requires a certain amount of concentration; you must put all distractions out of your mind and channel your energies and your thoughts to this one area. The process is difficult and requires discipline, but it may be the best way to extract this information out of yourself.

And be careful: sometimes the feeling is that "of course" you know your goals; you've always known them, so why bother putting them down? And that may be true; the right brain probably *has* had that knowledge. But for our purpose that's too dim and vague. These goals should now be clarified and set down on paper as specifics; that's the way to win this ball game. So if you have not yet been able to define those long-range goals that are of most importance to you, see if this method will help. Get a piece of paper and a pencil, draw some lines, and write! Two or four goals are okay, too; three is only a modest suggestion. Do what works for you.

The only thing of importance is for you to know: *What are your goals?*

If they're still not clear, let's try it yet another way: *I'll* give you the list. If you haven't yet been able to specifically state your long-range goals, or even if you have and you want to be sure you haven't overlooked something, take a long, hard look at this inventory; you're sure to find something on it you like. Look it over carefully, think about it, savor each value. Remember that the list is random; don't let the order of position influence you. First read it through, then begin to narrow it down. (Of course, please add anything that you feel is missing.) Put a check mark next to those values that really intrigue you, that you care about, that you cherish and esteem. Or cross out the ones that don't make it. Probably a good number of them will have some meaning for you; what you must do is try to narrow down this list so that you can end up with those goals that are of most importance to you, and have the most meaning. Try to limit your choices to only the most compelling; it will be easier later on if you do.

I strongly urge you to go through this step of putting your goals down somewhere. Trying to answer questions in your head often lets your response remain mushy; if you really want to profit from this, you've got to have the guts to be honest with yourself —and specific. So get out your pencil; don't waste—on top of all else—what you paid for this book. This awareness will be well worth the effort.

Again, don't be concerned about exact definitions of words or their relative meanings to anyone but yourself; this list is only for your use. As Humpty-Dumpty scornfully said, "When I use a word, it means just what *I* choose it to mean—neither more nor less." For example, I have listed "marriage." By this I mean the relationship, not the ceremony. And for some people, in this day and age, a five-dollar license isn't where it's at; they have their own form of the union which in old common law was called marriage and which today is known as cohabitation. So in working with this list, use "marriage" to mean the relationship as you view it, or as you use it. Or change the word; it makes no difference as long as you know what you mean—*and want*. And remember: these values should be *yours*; not those imposed by another, or by society. Think only of those values that *you* really care about; that is all that matters.

Here's the list:

Love	—	Pleasure	—
Power	—	Health	—
Popularity	—	Children	—
Marriage	—	Privacy	—
Prestige	—	Security	—
Leisure	—	Honesty	—
Independence	—	Freedom	—
Friends	—	Self-expression	—
Achievement	—	Recognition	—
Mobility	—	Belonging	—
Caring	—	Sharing	—
Dependence	—	Revenge	—
Religion	—	Success	—
Home	—	Recreation	—
Wisdom	—	Good looks	—
Wealth	—	Peace	—
Knowledge	—	Solitude	—
Individuality	—	Social Acceptance	—
Challenge	—	Serenity	—

So here you are, at a milestone. Hopefully by now you have achieved this goal: you know your overall goals. You may even know too many of them; narrowing down a list such as I've given you *is* difficult. The tendency (mine, too) is to want them all. And why not? But as you continue through the subsequent steps of making a decision and begin to use this information in a practical manner, on a day-to-day basis, you will find that it is easier for you to narrow down and focus in on your goals. Obviously the more selective you are and the fewer of these values that you choose, the better; the ability to concentrate on what is of most importance to you is a major factor in the fight to achieve it. For, just as obviously, the decisions you make that are governed by and designed to achieve these long-range goals will be good ones, and unquestionably will lead to greater happiness.

Now let's enjoy some more immediate desires.

Ah, the short-range goals: these are the ones I like. Instant gratification, pure hedonism, sheer pleasure! Live for the moment, the time is now. The present is all that counts. A loaf of bread, a jug of wine, a book of verse, and a charming companion—all under the shade of the sheltering bough, and the future is forgot, and the good life is now.

It would be nice.

And it should be so.

For, in fact, this orientation to pleasuring one's self is one of the more valuable purposes of these quantitative goals. The satisfaction of a new wardrobe, or even part of one; or furniture; or a vacation; or a new toy, like a camera or a ten-speed—these are very real joys that can give great pleasure for a considerable length of time. Goals such as these are an important aspect of our continuing life; they give it a certain substance and body that is necessary if we are to maintain sanity and achieve happiness in this world.

Living through the days and weeks—as opposed to merely existing—and making them more enjoyable is to me one of the more commendable of our desires, and I am fully in favor of this. There is absolutely no reason I am aware of why you should not have many such very immediate, very material, and very pleasurable goals; people who equate goals with sacrifice and restraint and self-denial are, at best, confused and deluded. Certainly, their "happiness" is based on a form of masochism.

For me, the short-range and pleasurable goals are more what life is really about than even the long-range ones. I'm a fatalist; I don't know if I'll ever get to all my long-range goals. But the more immediate ones are within reach and can be enjoyed constantly;

in this sense *everything* is today. *Carpe diem,* "seize the day," said the Romans; and, to a great extent, lots of people agree. I do.

All this is obviously fine and dandy, and certainly should be part of everyone's life style. And, by having these immediate goals in mind, your decisions that are determined by them, or help accomplish them, should be very easy. Your objective is clear; therefore your choice usually is simple: will it or will it not achieve this end? For, of course, that is exactly what short-range goals are: ends in themselves. At least, that's what *some* of these goals are; remember, there are also many that are building blocks for other, larger, and even long-range goals. But what could be better than gratification now while helping achieve a bigger objective as well? That's supersatisfying, and that's what you should try to do.

What I'm pointing out is very simple: I believe that any decision you make to satisfy a short-term goal is almost certain to be a good decision *as long as it isn't counterproductive to your long-range goals.* With this proviso, it becomes very easy to make these decisions. And the rule makes sense: everything you do should either give immediate gratification or help fulfill a long-range need. Or both.

I'll put it a different way: any short-range goal that is out of harmony with your overall qualitative objectives must of necessity lead to bad decisions. This is the crucial test, the question that—in effect—you must always ask yourself about each of your short-range desires: is it consistent with your long-range goals? For if the decisions you make on a daily basis are designed to achieve short-range goals that are counter to your long-range goals, or even to your intermediate ones, you are simply setting yourself up for eventual frustration and possible despair, usually without even knowing why. You must be aware of the dangerous possibility that short-range goals may divert you from your main objectives; they can too easily offer the immediate pleasure that then, unfortunately, turns into tomorrow's pain. Don't lose sight of the forest for the trees.

For example, a friend of mine was so enamored of the man who was currently in her life, and was hedonistically enjoying him to such a degree, that she gave no thought to her long-range goals.

She spent every weekend with this man, which she found very pleasurable; she impatiently passed the week waiting to see him again on Friday. But, after a while, she began to feel troubled and confused, and so she gave the relationship some serious thought. When she finally asked herself the crucial question of what she really wanted for herself, she was able to recognize the reason for her malaise: her long-range goals were marriage and family, two things that were not within his ken. And so she promptly ended that relationship. Although it was difficult to give up the immediate pleasures she was enjoying so much, she realized that her overall happiness was more important. By spending as much time as she was with this man, she was severely reducing her chances of meeting others, one of whom might be the answer to her dreams. Now she is careful to evaluate her dates more realistically in terms of her own more permanent needs, rather than her merely temporal ones; she no longer wastes her time on the one-night or weekend stands.

Another friend of mine was out of work and was considering two job possibilities. One of them offered a larger salary than the other, and this was tempting to him because he (understandably) wanted to have as materially rich and full a life as possible. But when he asked himself which of these jobs—or careers, since they both promised advancement in the future—he would be more happy in several years from now, he chose the second. Although the immediate monetary return was not as large, the greater psychological happiness he felt he would have in this field made the choice an easy one. Further, he was sure that because he liked this job more, his promotions would consequently come through more easily and more quickly than in the first, and so the salary differential probably would soon be equalized. Wisely, he did not allow the attraction of the immediate, short-range goal to mess up his more permanent objectives.

Once these people became aware of the conflict between their immediate desires and their long-range qualitative goals, and put their values in their proper perspective, they were much happier even though the superficial pleasures were temporarily diminished. So keep this simple rule in mind: your short-range objectives must not be opposed or harmful to your long-range goals; this is vital to making good decisions. Conversely, although your quantitative goals must be in harmony with your qualitative ones, you can have short-range goals that do not necessarily contribute to a larger goal but are, as I said, sufficient unto themselves. What is crucial is that the short-range objective does not interfere with, or jeopardize, or act at cross purposes with the long-range one.

And you have to be constantly aware of this; it is just too easy to compromise your long-range goals in order to achieve a very desirable short-range one. This can sometimes happen when you rationalize that "things will work out"; unfortunately, they rarely do. I know a couple who were very much turned on to each other, but they had somewhat different interests. She was a beach person, and he was country oriented, with a weekend home in the mountains. And he hated the beach just as much as she did the country. Her great desire was to live by the sea; he, of course, wanted to make the weekend home a full-time one. They spent several months of misery trying to convert themselves and each other to a mutual agreement on what they would eventually settle for in a home, but to no avail. Finally they realized that neither could give up their long-range desires and still be happy, and so they split. Now they are friends who have dinner together every so often—in the city. Sadly, neither of them had thought about their respective desires until they were in the relationship, and then it was too late; had they realized the importance of their long-range goals, the pain of the aborted affair could have been avoided. However, it was still easier this way than if they had been married, hoping that their love would overcome all obstacles, and then had found out that this panacea is nonexistent. The point is obvious: your long-range goals must always be the dominant factor in your life, and the earlier you clearly recognize them, especially vis-à-vis your short-term goals, the better.

In essence, all your quantitative goals—the short-range ones as well as the intermediate ones that may take "longer" to achieve—are bound to fall into one of three categories. Either (1) they will contribute to, and be instrumental in obtaining, the feeling of satisfaction that you get when you achieve your long-range, qualitative goals; or (2) they will simply be ends in themselves, giving you immediate gratification when you accomplish them, but having no bearing on the long-range goals one way or the other; or (3) they will be counterproductive and even damaging to your long-range goals. Clearly, only the decisions you make to effectuate the first two categories will be good decisions and, just as clearly, any decisions you make that carry out the third category have to be bad ones. With this approach to your problems constantly in mind, they should be easier to solve, and should be solved better.

I'm not going to be so presumptuous as to try to list short-range goals; such an attempt would be sheer insanity. The number is limitless; there is no way I could begin to cope with this and satisfy anyone, even myself. But I do think it would be of value for you to give some consideration to the more important of these objectives, and get some specific ideas as to what you want in the particular areas of your life. Take your job, for instance. Apart from what it may mean to you in terms of the future, and its career possibilities, what about it today? What do you need to satisfy you right now? Some people want a sense of security; others welcome a certain volatility that presents a challenge. Some want independence; others don't like that responsibility and instead prefer close supervision. How important is the immediate salary level? What do you feel are necessary work conditions? (I once, at a younger day, turned down an otherwise excellent job because it was somewhat out of the way and I didn't like the restaurants in the area. For some people, this reason may seem to be sheer nonsense; for me, it was the deciding factor.)

Here, too, it may help clarify your thinking if you list your requirements—goals, if you will—on paper, at least wherever you may be having difficulty. For example, a friend was in a relationship that gave him mixed joy and anguish; when he physically set down those attributes that he wanted in his mate he was shocked to realize that the object of his current affections had very neatly split the bill: there were just as many important, daily needs she did not provide as there were that she did. That was his dilemma: not enough. But once his short-range goals were defined and recognized, it became easier for him to make his decision as to what to do. Try it: somehow writing out even the short-range goals helps clarify them and gets you to understand them better. Here, too, you should be simple and direct in your wants; they should be very clear and very specific. Doing this is one of the best possible ways to determine these goals and their relative importance; knowing them will lead to better decisions all the time.

And once again, because I am obsessed with the importance of the idea (and you should be, too), I repeat that all these goals—the quantitative *and* the qualitative—must be *your* goals, and no one else's. Any decisions you may make to satisfy other people's ideas of what you should want are virtually destined to be bad decisions. You do yourself a grave disservice if you allow this to happen. The choice *must* be yours, based on your needs and values and goals.

For example, remember the story of the man in the sinking boat with his mother, wife, and child; the question was who would you save if you were that man? As I pointed out, most people choose either the child or the mother; the wife, poor woman, usually gets short shrift, almost as if this is not an alternative to be even considered. But one man I asked said, without hesitation, that he would save his wife, for to him she was unquestionably the most important of the three. I asked him why, and his answer was quite direct. His mother, he felt, was well past her prime and, in any event, bored him; his child, although lovable and loved, could easily be replaced several times over; but the relationship he had with his wife had taken him a bad marriage, several years of therapy, and countless meaningless affairs to finally achieve, and this meant more to him than either—or even both—of the other alternatives. And so his choice would be based on his own carefully thought out needs and desires: *his* goals.

If you fear that you may be substituting someone else's values for your own, go back to the chapter on the problems arising from a lack of sufficient self-respect; there you will find the clues to determine if it is happening to you. And if so, you know what to do. The relevant question to ask yourself all the time is if this goal is of value to you, and will it add to your happiness if it is achieved? That's all that's important. That's all that counts.

So it comes down to these several points, all of which are easy to remember and use. First, you must recognize the importance of continually having goals in mind in all areas of your life, even though they may be subject to growth and change. Then you must recognize the difference between your qualitative, overall, long-range goals that will give you a deep, abiding happiness and the quantitative ones that are oriented to the more immediate, hedonistic, pleasure-seeking desires we all have. Further, you have to be sure that the achievement of these daily desires is not counterproductive and destructive or damaging to the long-range ones; short of this admonition, virtually anything goes. Finally, you should be aware of how the minor, relatively inconsequential decisions and acts you continually make cumulatively build up to each of your larger goals, whether they be qualitative or quantitative. But the most important aspect of this—and the most important factor in making good decisions—is to know your goals and, in particular, the qualitative, long-range ones.

By now, I hope you do.

7

Recognizing Your Real Problems

A man I heard about, who had been in therapy for a time, suddenly stopped treatment one glum day. It seems that he was troubled by his psychiatrist's attitude: when he came early for his appointment, he was told he was anxious; when he came late, he was hostile; and when he came on time he was compulsive. Unable to bear the unending criticism, he quit.

Now, even if it did happen the way he relates it, this man was avoiding the honesty of his own feelings: his reaction was obviously an excuse to escape from whatever the therapy represented to him, and his reasoning was patently false and self-manipulative. In truth, he may have had difficulties with his treatment, but he was not dealing with the real problems that confronted him—the ones that brought him to therapy initially. And that's one of the major difficulties we all have in making good decisions.

Although it seems almost naive to say that the essential, basic step in making a decision is to know that a problem exists, to clearly understand what it is, and to want to do something about it, I think that this must be emphasized and not assumed. These are all vital factors in the decision-making process, and any mistake at this stage can be crucial, as it probably was for this man I've just described. Clearly, if you don't realize you have a problem, you certainly can't deal with it, and so you've lost the battle before you've started. Or if you don't define your problem properly, you may be wasting your time by "solving" a matter that is not the real cause of your troubles; this may be winning a battle, but it also loses the war. And, of course, if you don't want to do something about it—even if the something is consciously choosing to simply let it be—you've really capitulated to the enemy.

Very often it's a simple and clear-cut matter, one easily capable of definition, that requires a decision; having accepted certain situations in our lives, we must also deal with their consequent responsibilities. And most of the myriad problems we face on a daily, customary, and recurrent basis are self-evident. Beginning with the blatant interruption of your sleep by the alarm clock and the seductive question of whether or not to take five minutes more, virtually everything you do all day long requires a choice—a decision that must be made. It continues with the washing, and the brushing, and the dressing, and the breakfast, right through the day to the bed-time determination of whether or not to watch the tube for another fifteen minutes or so. All these actions demand choices to be made—or are the result of choices that were made at some point in the past. Simple matters, for the most part: which soap, toothpaste, and coffee got the nod? And maybe more difficult selections, too: remember my friend with the problem of the choice of tie?

Then to the office: whether to lie or not about being late (probably necessary if you took the five minutes), and if so what excuse to use (see how the earlier decisions set the need for subsequent ones?); what to tackle—or avoid—first; what should be done, or not. Write the memo, or not? Make the call? And what to say?

Who to lunch with, and where? Buy, or sell? Do, or don't? Decisions, decisions, decisions. All day long, all of varying degrees of importance.

Finally, home. *Always* a money problem: to save or to spend and, either way, what for? If you have children, there's also always a decision to be made about them. If you're single, there's the matter of who you're seeing, and (sometimes) why, and what to do in that situation. There are questions of clothes, and food, and recreation, and friends; what to do on weekends, and for vacations; problems of where to live, and how; and, of course, always the job.

We have accepted the routine presence of these matters in our lives, and we deal as best we can with the inevitable decisions they require. And since these are situations to which we are accustomed, the nature of the problems they entail is predictable.

Then there is another level of decisions—those which are thrust upon us by external events, whether we like it or not. A problem arises that we must deal with; to this extent we have no choice. The fellow who was fired from his job is just such an example; even though he himself actually triggered this situation by telling off his boss, he did not expect the reaction. Another example is the woman who was told that she was expected to immediately move in; she was not really prepared to face this decision when it was thrust upon her. Nor was another client, whose wife, to his surprise and amazement, decided on divorce; he had been certain his was a happy marriage. (His oblivion to his problems, as well as to her, was obviously a major factor in this woman's decision.)

Similarly, the ground rules of a situation you are in may change. I know of a couple who were living happily together, seemingly content in each other. Then, one day, the man announced that although he did not want to split, he did want to date other women from time to time. This certainly was a totally new set of conditions, and his young lady had to deal with this changed relationship and make her decision accordingly. Situations such as these, where you are made to deal with a problem because of someone else's actions, are only too clear and, also, impossible to avoid. They must be faced; something has to be done about them.

But not all problems are this directly brought to our attention;

there are many that are not caused by the open and specific acts of ourselves or others, but lie within us. They are the internal problems caused by our conflicting goals, or yearnings, or desires; usually they are emotional in nature and not clearly defined or thought out. However, we are often painfully aware of them, usually because of the inner turmoil they create. A divorced woman I know is in such a state of general discontent. She lives in a suburb of New York City because she feels it is a better place to bring up her fourteen-year-old daughter; consequently her social life is virtually nonexistent, as she is not interested in playing with the married men who surround her. She would love to live in the city proper, but what then of her daughter? And so the internal conflict goes on, while both she and her daughter are paying the emotional price of this war.

Whether we want to or not, we deal with the several types of problems that I've mentioned so far. And we do so actively and consciously. We cope with the daily, routinized ones; we struggle with the ones that are forced upon us; and, in a way, we deal with those that are deeper, and internal, and usually more emotional. Buying the usual brand of toothpaste is a positive decision, even if it is habitual; looking for a job is the same; so is the choice to remain in surburbia rather than move to the city. On a conscious, active level these matters are at least considered and then determined. And sometimes the situation is endured because of an inability or unwillingness to immediately deal with the problem; the clue to this, of course, is the phrase "One day I'm going to . . ." When you hear this, you know that a problem exists and is simply being allowed to continue, usually with a very reluctant, probably right-brain awareness of it. But no matter how they are handled, all these problems are being dealt with in one way or another. Even if the decision is to ignore or avoid the question, we are doing something about it by allowing the continuance of whatever the status quo may be.

One other group of problems is very common, yet paradoxically they are not being coped with at all. These are the issues we don't face up to because we don't recognize their existence. (Or won't. It's painful and embarrassing to say "I was wrong" or "I made a mistake." And so it's often a lot easier to just allow such situations to continue and avoid coming to grips with them.) And whether this ignorance is simply because of an inability to see these problems or a stubborn refusal to consciously admit to them, the result is the same: they remain alive and active, insidiously doing their damage and taking their toll. Often, we are unable to function properly because of them; even worse, we are invariably unhappy because of the inner unease they cause. For this reason, such unrecognized problems are very dangerous and therefore most important in our considerations. I'd like to discuss them a little so that you can become aware of them—and then, of course, deal with them.

There are various ways in which these lurking monsters spawn and survive. They may be the result of decisions once made; courses of action chosen that have now become habitual. Whatever the commitment may have been—time, money, energy, love—an inertia then sometimes takes over, and seems to blind the brain to the realities of the situation. Having paid the dues, we want to cash in on the investment. But in truth these matters are ripe for reappraisal; the loss you suffer by ending such a situation is undoubtedly smaller than if you continue to pursue yesterday's dream.

For example, I once had a job that provided marvelous benefits in terms of money and gifts; like many "careers" it had become merely a habit that I had spent a lot of time on and grown accustomed to. But it went nowhere. When I finally thought about why I wasn't happier in it, I realized that I probably could be doing the same thing for the rest of my life; it was a very comfortable rut. And that wasn't enough for me; it was therefore time for a change.

Sometimes, problems like this are allowed to continue because of laziness: "Why change it—it's working, isn't it?" is one of the warning signals in this kind of situation. So is "That's his job, not mine." Then there is the insecurity that results from tampering with the status quo: "It's too late to change now" or "We don't have time for it" are typical of this block. Or maybe it's a lack of ambition, or drive, or care; ennui can be extremely debilitating. Or the problem may be caused by unquestioning dependence on authority or the programmed patterns of the past, either of which invariably seems to result in an equivalent acceptance of one's fate, or at least a continual repetition of it. For example, a man I know has been married more times than he cares to remember; each woman, however, has behaved exactly the same in the relationship as all those who have preceded her—or will follow. For whatever reason, this man blindly repeats his past mistakes. And he will continue to do so, until he gives some serious thought to the question of "Why?"

Then there are those problems that we do not face up to simply because we are avoiding taking responsibility for ourselves; to grow up and accept adulthood can be very hard. Ego gratification is a case in point; remember the famous client I almost allowed to usurp my life? I was in trouble until I recognized both his nonsense and my needs, and then dealt intelligently with the problem. Or it may be that we are not really recognizing our goals and acting upon them; it may even be that we are behaving in a masochistic manner by succumbing to our fears and our guilts and doing what are essentially self-destructive acts. The family-oriented woman I mentioned earlier, whose husband exploited her as both a sex object and a maid of all work, was in exactly this pattern; so is the woman who continually pushes men out of her life, aborting what might be some very good relationships. This would be acceptable if the men were unworthy and deserving of her scorn, or if she consciously decided not to have a relationship. But she wants to get married, and some of these dates are really great; her pattern is not only unrecognized but is also a self-destructive one that can only lead to despair. Devices such as these, and all the other dangers we talked about in connection with gaining self-respect, can easily keep us enmeshed in the problems that we are not dealing with on any level. Obviously these are far more dangerous than the ones that come *pow*! at us, simply because they are so often overlooked and ignored while they continue to fester inside like a cancer. These avoided matters, therefore, are the ones that we must learn to recognize and deal with.

Your feelings are of enormous value in this recognition process; the emotional, intuitive right-brain reactions to your own life can be very revealing. An interview I once gave to a local paper touched on this and ended with the only quotable thing I said, at least for that day: "When you no longer look forward to the morning coffee, it's time to change the bean." The story is pertinent, for unquestionably the most sensible and easiest way to know if you have an inner problem is to keep asking yourself: How do you feel? What is your overall mood?

Do you wake up in the morning, looking forward to the day? Is there the excitement and stimulation in your life that makes you glad you're alive, and anxious to move, and do, and participate? Because if you're reluctant to get up and get out, that's another sign that something's wrong, that the world—or at least your small part of it—could be better.

Essentially, knowing if you have a problem goes back to that basic and all-important question: *are you happy?*

Now, as I said earlier, this can't be measured in any arbitrary, infallible way, but there are many things you can do, or look for, in your life that will give you an excellent indication that something's wrong and must be dealt with. One of my favorites is to learn to complain; the willingness to express your discontent is healthy, and often necessary. I don't mean you should become a painful bore to all your friends and acquaintances, a person clearly to be avoided; nor do I think that you must complain aloud. But you should at least learn to gripe to yourself, so that you can hear what's bothering you. I've learned more about my inner feelings by talking to my dog while walking alone with him in the woods than in almost any other fashion; the right-brain feelings can really come pouring out if only given the chance. Nor should you be hesitant to express your fears and your hostilities, even your anger. Sometimes the immediate, almost reflexive use of some basic street language in reaction to a particular event will be the best revelation of your real feelings, and a true indicator of a problem. (Certainly, if nothing else, it can help release the tension.) But any complaint, even if seemingly minor, should be listened to; your inner feelings can be an invaluable tool in helping you to focus in on problems that may be present, but are not really being dealt with.

Or are there warning signals? Is something telling you to watch out, that what you're doing is wrong, that it won't work? When this happens, some people say "the vibrations are bad"; I say that the right brain is working and sending its signals. There have been many times in my life when I intuitively knew that what I was doing was destined to be bad news; I could have saved considerable time and energy had I paid attention to these danger signals.

Take dates, for example. The chances are that you—as I—often go out with someone that we suspect will be wrong for us, yet in spite of this instinctive knowledge we waste ourselves by doing so anyway. Or on another level: I know a woman who had a fulfilling executive position with a large corporation; one day, however, the company was taken over by a multinational conglomerate. Things began to change, and, in retrospect, she now realizes that there were many times when she "kind of felt" her job was in jeopardy. But she did not give these feelings their proper due, and so when she was fired a short time later, she was totally unprepared for this blow. Contrast this with the woman who began to sense that her marriage was going sour; although she fervently hoped it would remain a good relationship, she began to think about the possibility that it might not. Therefore, although she did not expect a breakup, she was prepared for it when it happened—as indeed it did. (For those who are adherents of the school of positive thinking, I grant that attitudes may influence outcomes, but I believe that there is an enormous difference between expectation and preparation. I agree that if this woman expected divorce, she subconsciously may have contributed to it; however, I am convinced that she did not want the divorce but was simply—and wisely—accepting it as a possibility, so that she would not be caught unprepared.) What you must do is constantly listen for these inner warnings; *always* pay attention to your right-brain thinking.

Let's—for fun—start with the coffee. Do you generally look forward to it each morning? Have you thought about it at all—or, rather, have you really tasted it recently? (This, by the way, is exactly what I mean by habitual decisions: you may be buying a particular brand because you *always* bought that brand.) But of course this book is about more than coffee; I only ask this as a mock suggestion of the kind of self-questioning you need. However, it's essential that you become aware of yourself and your life; you must continually examine and question all your actions. Are you truly happy? For if you're not, it may be time for a decision. A big one.

If you're not quite sure of your feelings and need a little help in focusing in on them, you can use the left brain and a pencil to prompt the right by going over the list that follows. These are specific questions that, if answered honestly, will undoubtedly uncover the presence of problems you may have been reluctant to come to grips with; they may even help you to identify the source. Put the answers together into a comprehensive whole and the resulting insight is almost like one of those big amusement-park mirrors that show everything ten times larger than life; invariably they always seem to painfully focus in on all the problem pimples you've been wanting to forget.

In going through these questions, others that are more pertinent to you may occur; it is impossible for me to be all things to all people. The important thing to understand, and to look for, is awareness: these questions are only to help you find out if there is a problem and, if so, what it really is. I suggest that you write on a piece of paper the numbers 1 through 48 to correspond with the list below and put a plus (+), zero (0) or minus (−) next to each. Rate them so that the plus represents what you consider to be a positive, healthy reaction on your part; zero is a so-so one; and the minus an unhealthy one. And you must try to be brutally honest and totally objective with yourself; this is solely for your benefit and no one else's. You must be willing to see the acne; any fantasy that covers up the blemishes will hurt no one but you. Okay: let's go.

1. Putting aside the kidding about the extra five minutes, do you hate to get out of bed in the morning? Does the day usually seem oppressive, and would it really be great if you could avoid it completely? (A minus if you feel this way frequently)
2. Do you need, want, or get more sleep than your age and health warrant? (A minus for yes, often)
3. Or do you have trouble getting to sleep? (A minus for frequent insomnia)

4. Do you get stomach pains? (Frequently is worth a minus; ulcers should easily be several minuses)
5. Do you have a general feeling of discontent? (You've got the picture; I'm going to stop with these directions)
6. Do you get frequent headaches? (Doctors say that 90% of them are psychogenic)
7. Are you generally bored with life?
8. Do you feel suffocated?
9. Or intimidated?
10. Do you have a continual sense of loneliness?
11. Guilt?
12. Worthlessness?
13. Do you feel unappreciated?
14. Are you generally nervous?
15. Irritable?
16. Depressed?
17. Anxious?
18. Hostile?
19. Angry?
20. Do you cry a lot?
21. Do you have a poor appetite?
22. Or are you overweight?
23. Are you smoking more than usual?
24. Are you drinking more than usual?
25. Do you tire easily?
26. Are you overworked?
27. Are you unhappy in your job?
28. Are you overly sensitive?
29. What's your physical health like? (Constipation, diarrhea, any other maladies?)
30. Are you having nightmares?
31. Do you lack sexual desire?
32. Are you having trouble getting along with people?
33. Are you seemingly accident-prone?
34. Are you having difficulty in concentrating?
35. Do you seem to be making more mistakes than usual?
36. Do you wish someone was always by your side to tell you what to do?

37. Do you feel dependent on others?
38. Do you feel that no one really cares, that nothing really makes any difference?
39. Do you feel that you are compromising your goals or your values?
40. Do you feel that you're wasting your time, even your life?
41. Do you think that you have value, that your life has meaning?
42. Do you feel you're being imposed on, that people are taking advantage of you?
43. Are you settling for less than you deserve?
44. Are you generally optimistic about the future course of your life?
45. Do you have a feeling of pride in yourself?
46. Do you feel that you continually make bad decisions in your life?
47. Do you look forward to the future?
48. Finally, do you think that you are happy? Are you *really* satisfied with your life?

The minus answers you give to these questions are potential warning flags that signal stress and distress, and may suggest that an examination of your life is in order. There is no arbitrary rule of thumb that anyone can give you as to how to evaluate these numbers to determine potential trouble. I think, however, that if you have several minuses or lots of zeroes popping up throughout, you should recognize this as a symptom of a situation that requires attention—and the sooner the better. Of course, due allowance must be made for transient factors; obviously if you've just broken up with the most recent love-of-your-life your outlook is going to be gloomier than usual. But if the minuses seem to be indicative of your way of life, that's when it would surely seem that they should—and must—be heard, and attended to. It just doesn't make sense to ignore them.

There is another and possibly even easier way to recognize problems that you can look for—or, rather, listen for. And you don't have to do this at planned moments; you should be watching for this all the time. It is the use of the words "I should" or "I ought" or "I must"; whenever you do anything because you feel that you *have* to, beware. Know that this is the sure sign of a problem. Doing something because you are in some way compelled to do so, rather than because you *want* to do it, is an extremely important clue to indicate that you are in trouble, that your self-respect may be gone, and that you have an inner problem you are not facing. So, if you are doing a particular action because you feel you have to, really examine it closely. The odds are that this is a major causation factor of many of the minuses in your life, and it had better be dealt with.

An example of this distorted thinking happens with career jobs. I have heard people say that they "have to" remain where they are for "only" the next nine years in order to qualify for the pension; *then* they will be able to do what they want! Marriages that remain intact because one "has to" continue for the sake of the children are the same; the chances are that instead of ruining only the lives of the parents, the child is even more messed up than if an honest dissolution took place. The fact is that the child in such a situation often feels more guilt at having been responsible for holding a destructive relationship together than if he is told the simple truth that the two adults in his life are no longer as compatible as they once had been, and through no fault of his own. And by dealing with the problem openly and honestly, everyone concerned is far better off.

Even in the case of what seem to be externally caused problems you must be wary of a feeling of inner compulsion, so that you can deal with it accordingly. For example, a man I know was fired from his job for reasons that were not quite clear to him nor important to this story. Although he was single and had no financial responsibilities to anyone but himself, his insistence that he had to immediately find a job was so vehement that I felt it necessary to question him about his motives; the reluctant answers were not surprising. He is a product of one of the religious work ethics and had been brought up to believe that unless he was constantly doing something "productive," like holding a steady job in an office, he was a hopeless blight on society. The sense of shame he felt at being out of work was enormous. Yet what he really wanted to do—which I discovered when we started talking about his goals, and his desires—was to achieve recognition through self-expression; he wanted to write. And he had secretly and ashamedly thought to himself that it would be absolutely wonderful to take his unemployment insurance and some small savings he had, and go off for a while and try to create the great American novel. Of course, the guilt this aberrant idea generated was even more overwhelming than the simple matter of only being out of work, and he was literally tearing himself up inside because of this conflict. But what he *did* have to do, in order to achieve his own self-respect and consequent happiness, was to face up to his programming and his society and go off to his own form of Tahiti.

If you have been feeling discontent of the kind I have been discussing, or you have been doing things because you feel you must, you have a problem. Therefore, you must take a long, hard look at your life in each area of importance. Try to be as subjectively realistic about your status as you'd like a surgeon to be before recommending an operation. Measuring your present state of affairs against your own long-range goals, as you have already set them forth, how well are you achieving your desires? And what about your short-range goals? Is there something that—honestly—is really bugging you? And, for this purpose, don't confuse the issue by saying, "Yes, there is, but I don't quite know what it is." That's for later; right now I simply want recognition of the fact that there is a problem, even if it may be seemingly hopeless to explain. Think about your job/career situation, your family life, your social/sexual relationships. Are you as satisfied in each of these areas as you'd like to be? Or is there something that's been troubling you, that does require a decision on your part? This is a basic element in coping with your problems: you've first got to recognize that they exist. For when you know there is a problem, you can then get on to what it is.

Einstein said "the proper formulation of a problem is essential to its solution," and this is a bit of perception that is pertinent. For, having realized you have a problem, you must clearly understand what it is. That's the next step: you have to know it in its essentials. Decisions do become a lot easier to make, and are generally better, if you really clearly understand *what* it is that you must decide. Unfortunately, too often we accept the problem the way it is presented to us, or thrust at us; it's easier that way. Or we believe we understand it and therefore take it at face value, unquestioningly. But it's really quite easy to analyze it and understand it, and doing so can save a lot of later pain and turmoil.

You must get thoroughly familiar with your problems; you must dissect them and know them intimately. And you must do this whether the problem is external and caused by others, or internal and one you are first facing up to now. No matter its source, you must clearly comprehend the problem, in as simple and direct and blunt a manner as you can; at the same time you cannot oversimplify it and thereby leave out an important element. What you must do, in essence, is determine and carefully define the problem; there is absolutely no place here for window-dressing or sugar-coating. You must clearly know *what the problem is.*

I cannot overemphasize the importance of the word "what": it is crucial, not only here but throughout the whole process of decision making. Don't be put off by its apparent obviousness or simplicity: that's its danger, and its virtue. Don't take it for granted, or use it merely as a figure of speech. "What" is a word that demands specificity, and clarity, and simplicity in answer. It requires focus, and attention, and does not allow for vagueness or gobbledegook: properly used, it can eliminate a lot of garbage. And that's what it should do now. You must face up to its penetrating inquiry; you must respond to its probing insistence. You must ask yourself, the way all the brilliant defense attorneys on television do, the digging, delving, prying, searching, scrutinizing, piercing, inquisitorial question; you must confront the answer, and then pursue it and narrow it down, exhaustively dissecting it until you have refined it to its purest essence and its absolute truth. And I'm not kidding; you really have to get down to the nitty-gritty basic "what" it is you have to decide: you must cut to the core. For if you don't properly understand and formulate the problem, the odds are that you'll come up with a decision to match.

Problems requiring decisions almost invariably can be put into one or the other of two categories. One is the yes-or-no situation, where you must decide whether or not to take a specific action or do a particular thing. It might also be considered either-or: either you do this, or you don't. (Generally the "don't" is simply a continuation of the status quo.) The question is one that sets up nicely for this simplicity, and your choices are clear. Do you want to take this job, or don't you? Yes or no? There is no third way. Do you want to buy a condominium, or don't you? Do you want to get married or don't you? Do you want a child, or don't you? No "ifs," no "buts"; just very simple, very clear, and very clean.

Then there is the category that we can call multiple choice. Generally, in this situation, an action is called for and a choice must be made between two or more possibilities. There they are, the bunch of them, and you must pick and choose—but only one. But which? And, of course, the problem is often compounded by the fact that some of these are closely matched in their desirability, which means that not only do you have to decide on one, but you must also give up the others. Even if you have only two options to decide between, rather than several, making the choice can still be unpleasant.

Incidentally, you can legitimately say that even a "yes or no" situation is in reality a "which one," for it actually has two options—the one alternative of doing something, and the other of not doing it, even if the not doing it is simply the continuation of the status quo. In this sense, it too is a choice between two courses of action. Although in practice they are really treated the same way and so it makes no difference how you wish to refer to them, for the moment—and for simplicity in this discussion—I'll differentiate between the two. But the end result is the same no matter how you phrase it; you must clearly understand the question that you must decide.

There are also problems in which several decisions are involved; they are interrelated and one is dependent on the other. However, they are always some combination of these basic two situations of "yes or no" or "which one," and you must simply break the matter down into its essential parts, to be then handled on a step-by-step basis.

For example, a friend of mine was thinking about buying a new car and was trying to decide what to do. Here he was first faced with a yes-or-no situation: should he, or shouldn't he, make the purchase? Then, if the answer to this question was yes, that he did want (or need) a new car, he was faced with the problem of which one of the many availabilities on the market to buy. Or the situation gets compounded: another friend first had to decide whether or not to buy new wheels (yes or no); then if his answer was "yes," he had to decide whether he wanted a car or a truck (which one); and then he had to choose from the multitude of models (again which one, only further refined). Of course, had either person decided that he did not need new transportation, the matter would have ended with the first "no."

Sometimes, in such a sequence, the answer to one part dictates the next problem, which then has to be dealt with. For example, a client of mine wanted to move, for he needed more space, and he was offered a cooperative apartment. Upon talking over this possible purchase with his accountant and me, he realized that he first had to decide whether or not he wanted to own an apartment rather than merely renting one and, if so, was this one *it*? His answer was yes to the first question and no to the second; at this moment he is having great fun looking for what he hopes will be just right for his future needs. And these he now knows better than he ever did before.

Sometimes the "which one" comes first. Typical is a woman I know, who was trying to decide whether or not to marry a man she had become involved with, and who was now suggesting this serious commitment. However, when she carefully analyzed her feelings, she realized that she first had to consider whether she wanted to give up her autonomy and live with *anyone*. Which lifestyle did she want? This was the basic question to be resolved; once she decided this she could then deal with the other, if it was necessary. But it wasn't; she came to the conclusion that she really wanted freedom from commitment, and the independence that this guaranteed. Therefore the question of marrying this particular man became academic. Of course, had she decided that she *did* want such a relationship, she then would have had to face the question of whether this was the man she wanted to have it with (yes or no). In fact, she had two separate matters to determine, and the second became relevant only if she made a positive decision to the first.

So you must always be sure that it is only one problem at a time you are dealing with, and not an amalgam of related but independent questions that have become jumbled together. You have to get in the habit of asking yourself: is this *really* the question? Even if the problem merely feels strange, or doesn't sit right, be very careful: that's probably a right-brain warning of danger. And you will be surprised at the lack of clarity in the thinking of people around you as they tell you what they believe the question to be; sometimes you have to consciously and deliberately ask yourself: what is he *really* talking about? You have to listen to be sure that you really know what it is to be decided. You must always be sure to determine the basic issue, and separate it from the secondary ones; then decide each in order as—and if—necessary.

Should we try? Why not put down on a piece of paper a problem that you have been concerned with, or maybe one of those you were toying with earlier in this chapter, or even one that your self-questioning has helped reveal. Write it down so that you can deal with it as we go through the next steps. Make it a question that can be answered with a "yes" or a "no," or make it a "which one" inquiry. Use these two guides all the time, and the matter will be far easier to define, and clearer to understand. Make the statement as short as you can, and make it as direct and clear as the circumstances allow.

What is the problem?

If you are *still* not sure of what the problem is, there are some helps. Probably the best is for you to examine your behavior in light of your goals. To recognize these matters that require solutions, and to understand them clearly, you can match up what you are doing and what's happening to you against the direction you'd like your life to be going in. Posing this question can be a clarifying and sobering event, for you really see where you're at. And actually the process is simple: just ask yourself if you are achieving, at least in a general, overall way, your important goals?

There is a very practical way to make this examination; it is one that President Carter used in Georgia when he was governor, and that he instituted in Washington after his election. Called zero-based budgeting, it is based on the premise that you cannot take anything from the past for granted. On a regular schedule—annually, in the case of Georgia—each and every department and agency is reexamined and reappraised, to determine if it really is still necessary. Or, in fact, is it expendable, simply hanging on because of habit and inertia and even some backroom politics? Is it still productive? Is it efficient? Is it overstaffed and over-budgeted? How can it be improved, preferably without being enlarged? As the President described it, "It's a constant probing for a better way to do things, a constant assessment of priorities, and a constant winnowing out of the obsolescent or obsolete or moribund programs." In the same fashion, you must constantly and frequently ask yourself precisely that about all areas of your life: What are your goals? Are they being achieved? Nothing should be too minor, nothing too important, to be reexamined. If you're doing it, question it: make it prove itself. Start with the premise, for example, that you have no job; then decide what you really want in one. Stack this up against what you do have, and you may then more easily recognize any existent problems. Or try it the other way: Do you really like what you are doing? Do you get satisfaction out of it? And so on. . . . All to be answered "yes or no." In Georgia, many departments were scrapped; in your life—well, you may find this game fascinating. Or frightening.

Remember that the basic tenet of making good decisions, the most important factor of all, is to know your goals. Keep them in mind, and your problems will be that much clearer, and therefore easier, to deal with.

However, you may still be having trouble defining the problem; that's understandable. After all, many of these problems may have been buried and hidden for a long time, and rationalized away for even longer. Don't despair; there's still another way to get to the root of the evil. Why not play a game with your best friend, your closest confidant? Why not enlist his help, and ask what he thinks your problems are? Of course he must realize that his opinion is not to be judgmental but is merely for appraisal; further, if he levels with you, he must expect and be prepared for your shock and your hurt. And you must maintain enough humor and perspective to not allow his honest expression of possible concern to harm the friendship. Do the pain and anguish bit if you have to, but then use this information for your own good. Pretend—if only for the sake of this exercise—that his appraisal may be more objective and therefore more valuable than your own undoubtedly unbiased self-evaluation.

A word of caution here, however. Although it can be very helpful to get this friend's opinion, be careful that you don't also end up with his solution to your problems. You want his aid in the analytical area in order to help determine your problems, but you then have to deal with them on your own terms and for your own needs, not his. Also, be sure that what this friend is telling you is what he really perceives and not merely what he thinks you want to hear. If it's the latter, then he is doing you a disservice and wasting your and his time.

Finally, a word of hope. You have spent a lot of time in becoming more aware of your problems, and you may even have realized that you have some that were not too apparent. Don't be disturbed or depressed by this; it's really quite a healthy state of affairs. For, now that you understand more clearly what you must deal with, it will be far easier for you to make the decisions that do precisely that.

All that is necessary is for you to want to do so. And, obviously, you do.

8

How to Determine Your Priorities

Every problem you face is only one in the multitude of questions you constantly encounter each day. Each requires time and energy to decide—which, unfortunately, you have only a limited amount of at best. Therefore, you must intelligently fit this new matter into your overall scheme of things; certainly giving it the attention it is worth, but just as definitely not allowing it a place it does not deserve. You need to establish priorities: a system of preferentially rating the matters you have to decide so that they are treated in an order of importance and with a degree of care consistent with your sense of values and needs. And your priorities must conform to your goals; it's a simple matter of self-protection. Clearly, if you don't make the most efficient use of yourself and your energies in arriving at your decisions, you're the loser. Therefore, you will find great value in screening your problems in some way so that you can spend your time effectively: that is, use it to your best advantage and not waste it.

Certainly you cannot make your decisions the way you shop in a neighborhood delicatessen, where you take a numbered check when you come in and then patiently wait your turn to spend your money. You cannot attend to your problems simply in the order in which these occur, rather than with any determination of relative importance. It should not be "first come, first served." This is an attitude that sometimes prevails, seemingly based on the misconception that one is thereby demonstrating his powers of concentration, that he is not easily swayed or deterred, and that this devotion to ordered progression is a virtue. But to the contrary, I think that this is blindness, or at least myopia. Certainly, it is dumb. There is nothing sacred about any problem; if it is not as important as a more recent one, it should—and must—stand aside. New problems may be very demanding, even on the level of emergencies, or they may be relatively minor on your scale of values. You have to consider the immediacy and the importance of each one as it relates to you, and then you must position it in your overall scheme of things on the basis of your significant needs and wants and goals. That should be your only priority.

In a way, you must be very cold-blooded about your evaluation; you have to be both dispassionate and discriminating. It's similar to the wartime practice of *triage* (French for "sifting"), which developed because of a critical shortage of medical help. Under this concept, all casualties were put into one of three categories; within each group all were treated in kind. In the lowest ranking were those who could not be helped no matter how much attention would be given them. For these unfortunates anything beyond merely alleviating their pain was considered a waste; all they got were opiates. In the highest order were those who would get well through the natural healing process itself. Medical attention might accelerate this recovery but was not a necessity; consequently they too were merely treated to (and by) the pain-killers. In the middle were those who could not make it either way on their own: medical care was the deciding factor, usually between life and death. And so this group, the only one of the three that would clearly profit from the attention, got the priority; with not enough aid to go around, none was wasted on the other two groups.

You have to sort through your problems in the same way: you have to decide which are worth treating, and which are not. You have to choose very carefully those that deserve your immediate, conscious attention, and those that can be put aside. Of course, you should be aware of the possibility that in this process of selecting problems to consciously deal with, you may in fact be participating in an avoidance process. Therefore you must be sure that the emotional factors that can prevent you from facing up to a problem are not operative. The decision as to what to consider must be made on the simple basis of your priorities: what is the relative worth of the matter to you? That's all you really should ask. Rarely will you say to yourself, "Should I deal with this, or not?" People don't normally do the *triage* bit, picking some problems to treat and consciously discarding others. Rather, usually you face up to all of the problems that come at you, and often in the order in which they arrive. Therefore, your establishment of priorities should actually begin at this point—when you first recognize the problem. Any problem. It must fit into its place, before some matters and after others, based solely on the urgency and importance you think it warrants in relation to the others.

It would be great if you could even put all your problems in a sequential order, with the most important at the head of the column and the rest ranked in descending value behind it, each to then be dealt with in turn. Unfortunately, life is not that ordered and structured. Generally it is virtually impossible to isolate any one problem from all the rest and then concentrate on it solely, staying with it until it is solved—although this does happen occasionally when some crisis occurs and is the only thing you seem capable of thinking about at the time.

Usually, however, you must deal with many problems almost simultaneously; often a number of things vie for your attention, and just as often there are many that are actively in the forefront of your mind, forcing you to constantly shift your thoughts and your focus. Therefore you must have a clear idea of your more important and pressing needs: in effect you must constantly be aware of your goals. Only then can you maintain a proper perspective and ordering of your priorities; this is the only way you can be sure that you are devoting the optimum amount of yourself to them and not to less meaningful matters.

Further, you must proportionately allocate your time and energy; this must also be based solely on your needs and your goals. There is no valid reason why any problem should be given a certain predetermined amount of time that is measured out, equally, to all the matters that require your attention. Each problem must stand on its own; each must be treated alone, and with the relative amount of attention that it deserves, neither more nor less. For example, you may "love" a piece of clothing and think about buying it; the time this is worth in pondering is not the same as for the car you may also "love" for the same reason. Or deciding on where to spend a weekend is not worth the effort appropriate to a two- or three-week vacation. To occasionally bed, or not to, with a particular person isn't quite as vital a question as whether or not to also move in—at least for many in today's society. Gestation time *is* important, but it should be saved for the more meaningful of your problems.

The point is that you must, as part of your priorities, come to an evaluation of how much time and energy you wish or can afford to spend on the consideration and ultimate resolution of a particular problem, and then set a time limit on it that is consistent with its relative importance. You cannot allow yourself to get bogged down in the selection of a tie, or a towel; further, the chances are that neither will be that seriously noticed by anyone else. (Test it: think of your most recent business meeting, and try to describe that man's tie. . . .) Therefore, you should constantly keep in mind this sense of proportion—certainly giving to each problem its proper share of your time, but just as definitely not allowing it more.

Nor need you be concerned about the matters you have seemingly ignored—if you have done your selection process carefully. You will usually find that they are not really that important to begin with and, paradoxically, will be taken care of anyway. For the right brain, interestingly, will almost invariably decide them instantly; frequently it will do this just as well as if these matters had usurped conscious, deliberate left-brain time.

For example, I am constantly amazed at the amount of energy hordes of people expend in simply deciding where to eat and then, when they get there, on what to choose from the menu! Sometimes it takes on the aspect of a career decision, or at least a federal project. . . . Matters of this sort are really not worth too much time, and could wisely be left to the right brain. And should any such seemingly untended matter actually be or become a serious one, it will obviously insinuate itself into the group that is being consciously treated, to there receive its fair share of care.

The best use of time, and its proper conservation, is a relative matter: how much time a problem is worth is so subjective that there can be no firm, inflexible guidelines. But you do have feelings about this: you know (right brain, of course) when you are wasting time. There is a sense of stupidity, or frustration, or guilt that you feel; in such situations you know that you have played the fool. What you must do, consciously and arbitrarily, is to set a time limit on yourself. Fix a specific time parameter within which you feel comfortable, one that will allow you to arrive at a decision but is not too generous and therefore wasteful. For example, buying a few bath towels is probably not worth even a special trip to the department store but should be given, say, fifteen minutes during a larger, more meaningful shopping day. The purchase of a sofa, however, and the substantial investment that incurs, is obviously worth more of you; here you may spend a day and visit a number of stores to compare styles and prices. Within reason, you should try to come to a determination at the end of the time span you have allotted.

The resultant satisfaction when you accomplish a decision within the time you have set will make it all the easier as you continue to do it. It becomes a self-perpetuating process; once you get into the habit of fixing these bounds, you will soon find that you are doing this virtually automatically, and pretty much all the time. And as you become more proficient in making your decisions, you will also find that you can—and will—spend less time on many of these matters; that's great, and what good decision making is all about. So deliberately and consciously ask yourself how much of your time a particular matter is worth, and then do your utmost to live within that framework.

In a way, what it comes down to is that you cannot join the crazies of the world, to whom everything seems to be supercrucial; they really are quite funny in the pomposity of their own inflated self-importance. They have lost the ability—if they ever had it—to laugh at the world and its foibles, and also to laugh at themselves. Much of what happens in our lives is of importance to our happiness, but an awful lot of it just doesn't make that much of a difference. You've got to distinguish between the two and set your values and your priorities accordingly. That's probably the best test of all: how important is this decision going to be to you one week or one month from now? Judge it this way—and then govern yourself accordingly.

Of course, there are situations when you cannot take as much time as you would like for the consideration of a problem. You may run into such occasions when an inflexible deadline is imposed on you as an integral part of the decision; you may have to choose by a certain time. (That is, provided you *want* to deal with the problem in the first place.) Take, for example, a presidential election. You have to make your choice by a particular day, and no later; even if you're voting by absentee ballot you still must get it in the mail, or choose not to, by a specified date. Or another: the application for admission to a certain college must be in by a fixed, arbitrary date. These deadlines are immutable and intractable; no nonsense like "I'm thinking about it" is permitted. The day arrives, and the guillotine falls. So, to avoid such a beheading, you had better know if such a time limit is a factor in your matter to be decided.

Or you may face a more amorphous deadline, one that requires a certain amount of evaluation and involves an element of risk. You may like a certain model of a car that is on sale (or a particular used car which is, to that extent, somewhat unique); here you may be subject to an indefinite time pressure. If you delay your decision to buy—that is, if you take time to make up your mind—you run the risk of someone else coming along and buying it first. Procrastination can take its toll. Of course, you can try to get some guarantee of time in which to decide, such as by an option. A client of mine was considering buying a large parcel of land, and that's exactly what he did. By paying a few dollars, comparatively, he knew that he had the absolute right to purchase for a certain length of time. He thereby changed an amorphous deadline into an inflexible one; in a sense he simply bought time in order to get sufficient information to make his decision. So bear in mind if your deadline is not a fixed one but is uncertain, you will have to use your judgment to determine its relative—and real—meaning to you. You cannot succumb to the pressures of the salesman; conversely, you must be aware that if the item is good enough to interest you, it will also attract other buyers. Accordingly, you cannot take too long to act.

The rule here is simple: you should not, under any circumstances, give any matter more time than it is worth. You must constantly be aware of how much time the matter deserves, and then give to it that amount of yourself, but certainly not more. It would be criminal to waste your energies, and it is only you who is to blame if you do. Don't allow it to happen. Your time is precious; once gone, it's for forever.

You also need to consider one other aspect of priorities; it is what most people immediately think of when you use the word. This is the matter of your preferences. Preferences represent the distinction between what you like and what you like even more. Preferences are a knowledge of your needs and desires, evaluating between several of them that may be conflicting in such a way that you cannot have both. Therefore you must know your goals, and their relative degree of importance, for preferences are the priority you accord to each. They are the recognition of what is of more value and meaning to you at a given time and what is not; they are a realization that one objective sometimes has to be relinquished in favor of another. They are the knowing, and the awareness, of what you most want for your happiness.

For example, a friend has just called to tell me about several weekend houses she is considering sharing on Fire Island for the summer. The customary arrangement is for someone to rent a house with a number of bedrooms, and then to get a group of hopefully congenial people to join in the use of the place, sharing both its exorbitant rent and the inflated expenses involved. Almost always these places are geared to having "fun"; a nonstop social life from Friday to Sunday is unquestionably what it's all about. Sometimes, however, and depending on the group in the house, the atmosphere can be a quiet one, almost withdrawn and like that of a rest home; here, recuperation from the hectic week in the city is the need. The first kind has a certain excitement and exhilaration; one is always meeting new, possibly interesting people. The other is for rest and rehabilitation, and very little more. Of course, my friend would like—as would we all—the best of both worlds, but the houses available to her are clearly going to be one way or the other. And so, before she can start evaluating the individual houses and their occupants and choosing between them, she has to first consider her desires so that she does not waste her time trying to decide between apples and oranges. Therefore she must first determine her priority; on the basis of her needs and values—her goals—she must choose the area on which she prefers to concentrate her energies.

All this is what I mean by priorities. You must learn to put first things first; you must differentiate between what's important and what isn't. You must learn to save yourself; you cannot waste your energies on matters that don't really count, as compared to the bigger questions in your life. And you must also clearly recognize the relative values of the problems you do consider so that you afford to each the proportionate amount of your time and energy that it is worth. The price you pay must be compatible with the worth of the matter. Finally, you must know your preferences. You must be aware of your goals, both the long-range ones and the immediate ones, and you must recognize the relative importance of each so that when they come into conflict, one with another, you know which to give priority to.

How to determine all this? What can you do to make it crystal clear? Well, no one I know is in the habit of constantly sitting down and asking himself: Where does this problem fit? How important is it? How much time is it worth? What should I deal with first? What am I primarily looking for in this situation? That isn't how your decisions are usually made, nor am I suggesting it as a general pattern of behavior. You don't need to do this, for you already have most of this information; all you have to do is use it.

The knowledge is all up there, in the right brain, which continually is aware of what you should do, and when: all you have to do is listen. Pay attention to your feelings of what's important, of anxiety and concern—and then don't allow yourself to procrastinate. That's it. Almost always you *know* what you should be doing and what you most want, and you also know when you're wasting time or avoiding the issue; therefore, just do what this part of your brain tells you to.

However, there are times when this process may not be working as you'd like, and then you will find tremendous value in consciously making a careful analysis of your priorities. Sometimes the knowledge that your life is organized into some form of logical order can give you a sense of peace and security that in itself will help make your problems far easier to handle. You'll find this especially true when you are feeling both confused and pressured; there are times when all of us are under such mental strain that we seem to be on the verge of a nervous breakdown and any relief is welcome. Certainly you've gone through periods when you just want to scream and escape from everything; I believe that this happens when the right brain becomes so overloaded that it virtually short-circuits, and nothing seems to make any sense. That's when you should use your left brain to bring order to the chaos; that's when the natural balance of the brain can restore equilibrium to your life.

Actually, you can do so quite easily. Just get a pencil and a pad of scratch paper, sit down in a quiet spot, and write down all those things that you feel are bugging you, or that you should be facing up to or taking care of. Make the list as complete as possible; you should include everything that is on your mind, whether big or little. Just put it all down without any regard for the relative importance of each item. Then, when you have completed the list, and everything you think you should be dealing with is there before you, rank all these matters in order, based only upon the degree of your concern. Which, of all the items you have listed, is most important to you? Take your time to think about and weigh each one; spending time here can be extremely worthwhile. And be careful: an apparent first choice may be that only because of the past, patterned baggage you live with—your programming, your fears, your insecurities, your guilts.

In doing your ranking you must carefully consider your goals, and especially your long-term ones; they, more than anything else, will help bring clarity and sense to this matter of priorities. For example, a client of mine was involved in a number of projects, some of which were financially rewarding and others of great ego gratification. Both goals were important to him. But he was beginning to feel suffocated by the pressure of having to continually perform his genius act on each of the many deals he was involved in. And so, one night after dinner, he decided to do this evaluation and began a list of his priorities. He was immediately appalled at the sheer number of his projects; no one, he realized, not even he, could successfully deal with all. Further, in the attempt to juggle this horde, he was neglecting his family; this, his wife quite bluntly pointed out, was not only unfair to her and their children but could easily lead to divorce. More than anything else, my friend is a family man, and his wife's evaluation shook him up; "family" got the number-one position on his list. But then, by ranking the other matters, he realized where he had been spending an inordinate amount of time in relation to his real priorities. Situations that were of relatively little importance in his overall picture had been receiving more time that they were entitled to; they were now—in his own form of *triage*—struck from his list. Or, rather, they were removed from his personal list and delegated to subordinates; each of these matters, he felt, could be reported on to him by these others in a comparatively short time and therefore need not deter him from his personal priorities.

You can deal with even relatively insignificant problems this same way. If you have a mess of calls to be made, or letters to be written, or chores to be done, you can list them all and order them. No matter is too insignificant; nor does such a list have to be of great consequence. The point is that this method of ordering your priorities is a form of relief valve: you do it only when you have to, when you feel the need to get order and clarity into your life, and when you want to do it. Then, as you take care of these matters and tick them off, the weight that is lifted because the more im-

portant things are accomplished makes the others much easier—
and faster—to also accomplish. Try it for yourself and see.

This method of establishing your priorities can also work in
terms of your goals, especially your short-range, quantitative
ones. *Before* seeking a solution you can make yourself fully aware
of the relative importance of the needs you want to satisfy. A
woman I know, who is a very successful investment banker,
makes this analysis for her relationships; it's much like the way
she advises her clients on their securities. Her long-range goal is
marriage and a family, and she understandably wants to be sure
that the crucial bottom line is in black ink, not red. Therefore, she
has made a list of all her specific requirements for a happy relationship, and has very carefully given them priorities. Having
done this *before* meeting a man, she is able to efficiently separate
the viable and datable possibilities from those who would be only
of short interest. A quick drink, and she knows precisely the potential of the bond.

Another example of this kind of prospective analysis was prac-
ticed by a client of mine who had to hire a new assistant to replace
the one who was leaving. My client had interviewed a number of
people for the job, had narrowed the field down to a few, and was
now finding it difficult to make a choice between them. However,
when he listed his requirements for the position and then ranked
them preferentially in terms of his priorities, his decision was
easy; one person clearly excelled in the most important of these
qualifications. Probably any one of the people he was considering
would have done a good job; however, by going through this
procedure he certainly increased his chances of obtaining the best
possible man for the job. This method also helped him save much
valuable time in making his selection; by using it he was able to
deal with the problem very effectively and very quickly. That's
one of the big advantages of this system of logically ordering your
priorities: it keeps you from procrastinating or spending too much
time on any given matter.

So there you are—your priorities: the relative importance of all
the things in your life. It's the order in which you deal with them,
and the amount of time that each is worth, and the awareness of
what your preferences are. Which, of course, is what I have been

saying one way or another all through this book, and is really the most important priority of all: you've got to know what you want for yourself. You've got to take care of you.

It's very easy. And it makes sense.

9

How to Develop
Your Options

While I was writing my book on backgammon, one of the editors called me about some matter; in the course of the conversation he asked me to tell him how to play a certain opening. I asked him what his usual move was when he got this particular throw of the dice. "I go to the bathroom," he said, "just to get away from it." I told him what I recommended, and asked if he had ever played it this way. "No," he said, "I never thought of *that*."

Of course, that was his difficulty. For if you don't think of something as a possible course of action—an option, if you will—you certainly can't choose it as the solution to your problem; clearly your final decision can be no better than the best of the alternatives before you. You've got to know that the alternative exists in order to consider it and then, possibly, decide on it. But without being aware of *all* your alternatives, you may very well overlook the one that is the answer to your dreams. Therefore it would be ideal if you are certain you know all of your possible options; surely this knowledge would guarantee far more comfort when making your decisions. You would then at least be secure in the knowledge that this best alternative *is* included among those you are considering and is not being overlooked.

Although my point may seem obvious, I emphasize *all* the alternatives because too many people tend to assume that making a decision is merely to choose between two things, thereby overlooking the pertinent fact that often numerous options are available to them. One constantly hears the phrase "Look at *both* points of view" rather than "*all*." Similarly, most people assume that the horns of a dilemma never number more than two. However, it can happen both ways: you will recall that in essence every decision falls into one of two basic categories. One is the simple either-or situation: you can either take the action of making a change, or allow the status quo to continue. For example, you may be offered a new job. Do you take it, or do you stay in the one you now have? In a relationship: do you split, or stay? Or if you want a relationship: is he or she the one, or are you better off remaining single? Decisions such as these *are* pretty much yes-or-no matters, and can generally be treated with apparent simplicity. In the other situation, where you have a particular goal in mind, you must choose from among several possible courses of action to properly satisfy the need. Here it is somewhat more complicated, and you must be careful that you have not oversimplified the situation and thereby overlooked some options; you must be as sure as you can that you've got them all.

There is another reason why you should want to know all your alternatives. Studies have shown that more people suffer a feeling of helplessness when they do not think they have a freedom of choice. And this belief can be so whether or not the dearth of alternatives is real or only imagined. The perception of the individual is of moment here, rather than the actuality of the situation he is in. There are even unfortunates who sometimes are unable to perceive any choices; pathetically, they truly believe that there is absolutely nothing they can do. I know of a man who was so totally overwhelmed by this feeling of desperation—he was a principal in a failing business, in which all his life savings were invested—that he seriously contemplated suicide. He saw no way to save the venture, and bankruptcy was a disgrace he could not bear; he actually thought death was preferable. Fortunately, he was able to get some sound advice which, by suggesting other possible courses of action he had not discerned, relieved the pressure he felt. His panic had come from his mistaken belief that he had no viable alternatives; this kind of irrational response to the feeling of being trapped is understandable, and frequent.

And this feeling of helplessness can sometimes be just as frightening and frustrating even when there is an apparent either-or choice, but the perceived alternatives are not fairly well matched. In such a situation your feeling of being boxed in and suffocated may be as strong as if there is no choice. If this should happen to you, be sure that you have properly defined the problem, and that you are cognizant of all your options; as I pointed out earlier you must always be wary of these dangers.

For example, the wife of a professional army officer I know often found herself in such a situation; she felt she had no realistic control over her life because her husband was being stationed in different NATO countries in Europe. She had to go with him, wherever he was sent, for she did not wish to leave him. For her, there seemed to be no alternative. But the real question she had to face was not whether she had to travel with her husband or leave him; she had to decide how else she could improve her situation. They talked about it and finally bought a house outside their favorite city, which had a military airport nearby. Now he "commutes" regularly to where she has established roots. Although she's not with him as much as she'd like, the marriage is intact and healthy.

In terms of a progression on a comfort scale, the worst predicament is the one I've just discussed, where you perceive no choice. Since you can do nothing except what seems to be the one practical course of action, it is very easy. In fact, no decision is necessary. But in such a case you are hopelessly trapped and usually dangerously unhappy. The next step up this ladder is to have two alternatives, but of unequal value. Here you are not much better off; again the selection is practically forced upon you. Then there are two choices, of roughly equivalent merit; here, at least, you have the opportunity to select—and so a sense of freedom begins to emerge. But to have several alternatives, all valid and closely matched in desirability, makes it more interesting. Maybe harder, in that it now requires some thought—and even work. But now you have the possibility of a real choice, and so the sense of freedom is greater; there is nothing more welcome than the feeling of being your own master. And since this situation also radically improves the prospects of actually being better satisfied, the process is therefore in fact more comfortable. And the larger this number—up to a point—the happier one generally is; often there is even a certain enjoyment in such circumstances, and this consequent lack of pressure can in itself further help achieve a more successful outcome.

However, there is no magic number of alternatives that will make one happy. This point of satisfaction—if it can be called that—varies for different people. For some, the right number is small. A woman I know lives in a cramped apartment; each year, when her lease is about to end, she begins looking for something new. And each year the scenario is the same. She likes something she sees, and she begins to have fun in the planning of her new pad. Then she hears about another apartment that is available, goes to see it, and likes it too; indecision begins to set in. She should have stopped at the one alternative. Then, in an attempt to resolve the dilemma she runs to see anything else she may hear about, or is advertised. But too much! The confusion panics her and she can't decide which to take; she feels sorry both for starting the whole mess and also for herself. Of course, the one time she did make a decision, it was too late because of her procrastination; the apartment was gone. So she remains where she is, and where she has been for too many frustrated and unhappy years.

But her situation is not the usual, and indeed it is also far from the norm. Most people feel more comfortable with three or four alternatives than they do with two, and even five or six are welcomed by many. However, as the number of options increases, the law of diminishing returns also sets in; too many alternatives progressively lead to confusion, discomfort, and even migraine. It's like living in a department store—you'd never know which chair to sit in. And so, often, when there is such a plethora of choices, you don't do anything at first; inaction is the initial reaction or, as with my apartment-seeking friend, even the end result. But this immobile state is generally followed by what may seem to be an impulsive decision—though, of course, it is probably only the right brain taking over.

However, in order to make your best decision, it doesn't matter how many alternatives may be ideal for you. You must first get *all* of them in hand so that they can later be considered and evaluated. Even those alternatives that don't seem to be quite on a par with others should be collected at this point; they may be more valid than you at first think they are, and they can also trigger your thoughts toward other possibilities. This step of collecting alternatives should not be judgmental in any way; *all* suggestions of possible courses of action should be welcomed, no matter what their apparent worth. Later you'll make the list into a workable, manageable size; for now you must be sure you clearly discern and discover all possible alternatives that are available to you. Don't fear—or permit—the possibility that you will later feel, "If only I had thought of that. . . ."

It also is important to find alternatives that allow you a positive action rather than only negative choices. To have to decide between the lesser of two evils is neither comfortable nor fun, and such a decision is often avoided. And having only negative alternatives can also increase whatever feelings of despondence or frustration that may have been occasioned by the problem itself. I remember watching a television program on which five women were being interviewed; each was married to a man who constantly beat her up. Each had left her home several times, and for different reasons each had returned every time she left. They all expressed the same despair: they had no alternatives. Or, rather, they had no *positive* alternatives. On the one hand, they had not been able to exist in the outside world, for various reasons; on the other, their home lives were unquestionably terrible. Neither alternative was really palatable. Fortunately, the purpose of the program was to give them a third—and positive—alternative. Money was being appealed for, to fund a halfway house where these women—and others like them—could find both protection from their crazed husbands and also get sufficient financial and emotional help to start life anew with some chance of making it.

Admittedly theirs is a severe situation; the point, however, is valid even when the circumstances are not as stark. For example, I know many people who chose not to vote in the last presidential election because they believed that neither candidate offered a positive choice. However, most of them had a certain feeling of shame at having abrogated their franchise. Clearly, they would have preferred either a third candidate, or at least a lever that affirmatively said, "I'm voting, but not for anyone." Positive choices *do* make life a lot easier, even if only to relieve guilt; you should strive to find them.

In essence, that's the ideal: a larger, rather than smaller, number of alternatives, all relatively well matched in value and positive in nature. That's what you should try for if you want to be in the best possible position to make a good decision.

The best way to determine some of the more important and more valid of your possible alternatives is to return to your goals, preferably your long-range ones, and use them to obtain some perspective on where you are, especially in terms of where you want to go. Looking at your problem in relation to your overall needs and desires, you should be able to come up with a pertinent option that conceivably can be the solution to the situation—or at least contain the germ of the cure.

Ask yourself what it is that will make you happy. Don't allow yourself to think of what you "should" do. Think of where you want to go and what you want to do with your life; then think of the ways in which you can accomplish your goal. Each of these *ways* is another alternative; one of them, more than likely, will be the best one for you. In a sense, this procedure is like using a road map: knowing that I wanted to ultimately get to Phoenix, it was easy for me to find several detours—alternatives, if you will—whenever I came upon construction or some other problem along the road. It's also like the woman who joined the Peace Corps, or the fellow who decided to write a book. These alternatives didn't become apparent to them until they thought of what they really wanted. Then they were able to recognize the possibilities that had been hidden from their consciousness and do something constructive about them. Do the same: use your goals to give you a point of view about your problems. You will find that usually this is the most effective way to come up with the best alternative possible.

We always come back to our old standby: when you begin to think of what you want for yourself, a number of promising alternatives will be very apparent. Too often, we stifle or sublimate the emotions we are experiencing and thereby bury a major source of honest, valid and meaningful alternatives that are available to us. This inability to ask for ourselves also goes back to the whole matter of lack of self-respect; we are so afraid of rejection, and so programmed to be stoically undemanding and "unselfish," that we frequently and automatically close off the possibility of emotional alternatives and never even consider them. We have been trained not to say: "I want . . ." or "I feel. . . ." But very often that is exactly what we must say.

If we are to avoid frustration and allow ourselves our most valid alternatives, these feelings have to be acceptable options that we are willing to use if we choose. One of the most pathetic of the various stories I hear is the recurrent one of the women who rarely, if ever, experience an orgasm; it is appalling how many females fake the response because they are unable or unwilling to say that they are not satisfied. Look at what they are missing because they refuse to allow this alternative, and ask for what they want. Sometimes, of course, under these circumstances the woman may fear the man will feel castrated by this "demand," but isn't this actually his problem based on his lack of self-respect? It then really comes down to a question of her priority: should she take care of him, or of herself?

Very often, when you think of what you really do want for yourself, you should come up with what may be the most important alternative of all: what you don't want. I call it the option of No. That's it: just "No." Or "No, I don't want to do—" whatever. "No, I'm not interested." "No, thank you; please leave me alone." This should be the answer to many of the demands made upon us (by others, as well as by our training), and should be kept in the forefront of your mind so that you automatically consider it as a valid alternative, almost before you think of anything else.

I am troubled to see how often people do things that they absolutely do not want to do; they just find themselves unable or unwilling to say, simply, "No." Often the clue to this kind of masochistic behavior is the use of our old friends "I have to" or "I should" or "I must." These phrases are the danger signals that indicate your inability or unwillingness to think out your desires and needs; they are the programming of your youth. Of course what you must do is *not* obey these imperatives. Instead, challenge them. The freedom of not "having to" is often one of the most appealing alternatives of all. So whenever you find yourself thinking or using one of these compulsory phrases, first say, "No," and then ask yourself instead "Why? Why not *this*, or *that*, or whatever?"

You simply have to be willing to examine society's rules of conduct by your standards and decide what it is you want for yourself. You should not, and cannot, accept as the only alternatives those which society (or some part of it) tells you are permissible and insists you restrict yourself to. For example, a woman I know wanted a child more than anything else in the world; she felt she would be an excellent mother and that both she and the child would benefit. However, try as she might, she could not find a man with whom she felt she could have a long-lasting relationship. She was not willing to make the sacrifice of marrying a lesser light in order to have a father for her child merely because society said she "should." However, when she examined her needs and questioned her assumptions, she realized that she was perfectly capable of not only supporting herself and the baby, but she was also willing to ignore the dictates of society and (for her) its antiquated morality. She thereupon set out to find the best genetic father that she could, rather than a husband. When she did, she contrived to become pregnant by him, although unbeknown to him so that he would not feel any subsequent responsibility. And so she now has her child but does not have to pay the price of an unhappy marriage. This woman's decision may not be yours, but the point is clear: you must learn to challenge all the patterns of behavior that you had previously been willing to accept. You must learn to want for yourself. This is not only an acceptable but also a desirable alternative. At least, it is one you must consider.

Another emotional alternative you should consider is trust. The lack of it in our society is so prevalent as to be frightening; we are becoming increasingly insular in our lives and lonely in our hearts because of our inability and unwillingness to trust another. But the alternative of trust is vital to many problems we must deal with; without it we are so restricted in our choices that our decisions have to suffer. We should not, of course, give blind trust— for, at times, cynical distrust is even more called for—but the element of trust is a necessary factor in almost everything we do. Our relationships, our jobs, even our family lives revolve around this essential. Not to include it in the realm of possible alternatives is to severely limit oneself.

For example, I know a man who will not marry again, having been badly burned on his first try. Nor will he live with a woman or give her a key to his apartment, for fear that she is going to "take" him. As long as he feels this way he will live behind a barricaded wall, and he surely will live in loneliness. Similarly, an actress I know will not trust any of the directors she works with, believing herself to have been "used" by one early in her career. She mentally resists their suggestions and even, in an attempt to assert her independence, openly fights them; the net result is that without their help she is not as good as she might be and, further, she is getting fewer and fewer job calls.

As for the matter of love as an option, that's the subject of at least a whole other book; of course it is closely related to, and a direct outcome of, the bigger subject of trust. And the point is the same: you must feel love, and you must express it. You must allow it to be a valid alternative when necessary or desired.

But the one emotion of which this is especially true is anger, the feeling that we experience more than any other in our insensitive society. It is also the one that, in our equally "civilized" society, we hide or cover up more than any other. We are specifically trained to not allow this emotion in ourselves; we have forgotten that anger is a perfectly natural feeling. And when we do feel it we also instantly pay an enormous price in guilt, almost as if what we are experiencing is highly immoral. Even more, we certainly don't entertain the thought of acting on our anger if we should feel it; this alternative is aborted before it is born.

I think this way of reacting is a mistake. I think that anger—or hostility, rage, hatred—call it what you will, the underlying feeling is the same—is an honest, true, and necessary reaction to many of life's problems and a most desirable alternative to have in one's arsenal of potential weapons. I do not mean that uncontrolled rage is to be condoned; I think that Benjamin Franklin's line "A man in a passion rides a wild horse" is very appropriate. The restraint should be in the way the anger is handled and controlled, so that its expression is civilized and not destructive. But feeling anger and acting on it is a basic need that should not be denied. Confrontation clears the air, and often the relationship is better for it. Therefore, I strongly believe that this emotional release is a very valid option, and one that you must be aware of and willing to utilize when necessary; the saying is, "A good hate a day without guilt keeps the psychiatrist away." The ability to tell someone off, and not feel guilty about it, is a very healthy one; even the punching of a symbolic pillow can help serve the purpose.

Just don't hit *him*. (Or her.)

The difficulty comes when you don't allow yourself to feel the anger, but instead try to "understand" the other person's problems and "accept" that person for what he or she is; the result too often is that in doing so you wind up with an unacceptable compromise that merely prolongs the basic problem from which you have been suffering. Think about it: any time you have been involved with another person who has hurt you, wasn't it a lot better for you, and easier in the long run as well, if you were able to tell him your feelings? Anger shows concern, and it can be coupled with any other emotion, such as love; when anger is used as an alternative in a relationship its primary function is to restore honest communication. And this it does very effectively. Sometimes, for other and valid reasons, anger cannot be the choice you make, but it will be of enormous help emotionally if you at least consider it. (And *then* hit the pillow. . . .)

And don't depend only on yourself to find your alternatives: ask friends or family for their thoughts. Don't ask or look for advice;

people (even those close to us) often hesitate to accept such a responsibility, and this may inhibit them. Conversely, they may *love* to give advice—and never stop; often such opinions are good for their problems, but not for yours. So ask only for their suggestions of possible alternatives; one of them may perceive an option of which you, for a variety of reasons, may have been unaware. Maybe you'd even like to have a few people close to you come over some evening for a brainstorming session; this is a kind of kinky way to solve problems that sometimes works. The method is not successful for all matters, or even many, but in some cases it can be an extremely helpful way of finding alternatives that are really way out. It's sort of a game, and ideally it's played with up to five or six players. You state the problem to the group with as much specificity as possible: "How do we peel these potatoes faster?", for example. Then, as quickly as possible, everyone tries to come up with wild, imaginative solutions to the question, just as you do in charades. Each alternative should be jotted down, even if by a one-word key, so that all can be remembered later; and every one of these suggestions should be given this treatment, no matter how crazy they may seem. That's the object: *quantity* of ideas, not quality.

One of the basic rules of this game is there must be a total suspension of judgment, both of approval and disapproval, while it is going on. No one is to say that something is a good or bad idea; you don't want to slow down or stifle this process by evaluating now. Even more importantly, you want the mad ideas to trigger others that, though possibly coming out of left field, may nonetheless be absolutely right. That's another rule: the participants should not only accept an insane idea when it is presented but also try to improve on it by adding to it and changing it, even becoming wilder and more flagrant in their contributions until their responses just may erupt into something that works. Nothing should be dismissed or overlooked. What you are trying to do is turn on and turn loose the right brains of all those playing the game. And, as I said, for certain problems it really works. (Incidentally, beer—or whatever similar you fancy—helps.) The wild diversity and sheer imagination of the answers—"Peel them with a chain saw" or "Train an octopus"—can make you laugh, but they also may lead to a better way, a more viable alternative than any you previously had. And if not, at least it's a good excuse to get together with some old friends.

The point is that there *are* ways out of dilemmas; you simply need to approach the problem imaginatively so that alternatives can be found—or even manufactured—so that you can have more and better options to choose from when you have to make a decision. The essence of brainstorming is to reject, at least for the sake of examination, the present point of view.

But you do not have to go this full route with the whole social gathering; you can do it alone. The most valuable aspect of brainstorming is that you pretend that all the ways you know to solve this problem are obsolete, or impractical, or no longer exist—and so you ask yourself what new, unthought-of, and untried ways can you come up with, now that you must? The procedure forces you to change your approach to the matter; you have to alter your point of view. You have to speculate from scratch and look for more than the apparent; you have to re-examine your concept of the problem. Think about it: what *would* the alternative be, for example, if you did an absolute about-face from your present course of action? That solution just might not be so crazy; at any rate it certainly is worth examining.

For example, again consider the fellow who has gone off to write. Had he, instead of examining his goals, considered the possibility of *not* getting a job and thought of the alternatives based on that course of action, he probably would have come up with the same answer. Being willing to attempt a new point of view, even a total change of direction, can really make you think and possibly find some interesting new alternatives. The young girl who was verbally insecure and instead "wrote" her composition on the piano did exactly that. This shifting from the expected to the unexpected can often be the solution; in this case it really was a good one, even if her teacher was not quite ready for it.

Another example is that of a carpenter I know who had trouble collecting his bills on time. He thought about adding an interest charge to the bill if there was an unconscionable delay before he was paid. He realized, however, that doing this would probably antagonize a good number of his customers, and so he decided against it, suffering instead the frequent frustration of waiting for his money. But then someone suggested to him that he increase his bill slightly and offer a discount if he was paid promptly! That is, if he felt he was entitled to $80 for his work, he would send his customer a bill for $89, with a notation that $9—more than 10 percent—could be deducted if the bill was paid within 15 days. Of course, his novel approach to bill collecting worked like a charm: since he had to be paid sooner or later anyway, most people wanted to take advantage of this not insubstantial saving. And, if they didn't, he got his interest instead!

You might also try changing an element in the situation, or in some way shifting or altering the emphasis. Remember the man who had trouble selecting a tie to wear each day? Someone suggested to him that he eliminate the problem by wearing turtlenecks instead of shirts that required ties. Not only did this alternative solve the matter for him but it also got him started on wearing sport jackets and slacks, providing an image that he now enjoys more than his previous, buttoned-up one.

Similarly, you may try substituting one element for another seemingly fixed one; the alternative may actually be better. For example, a woman I know who was most desirous of having a long-term relationship was continually being hurt in a series of affairs; for whatever reason she just didn't get along with these men for any length of time. She also realized that her friendships with women were generally far deeper, and far more rewarding, than any she had with a male. Consequently, one day, she tried a new alternative: she had a homosexual affair. And you guessed it: today, still in it, she's very happy. By merely switching genders in her search, she changed her whole life. A man I know did the same thing in his career. He found that he did not get along very well with other men in business, and he was constantly unhappy because of this. His sister, who recognized the problem and also was aware of some of his talents, remarked on it to him; today he is thoroughly enjoying a position of eminence as a women's hair stylist.

A compromise between two seemingly unattractive alternatives may also offer a way out. By taking certain aspects of two or more possibilities, and combining their advantages, you may be able to find a reasonable solution. For example, a friend's daughter wanted to go to a prestigious New England college for various reasons; unfortunately, the school was considerably more expensive than a less-known one at which she had also been accepted. And so the family arrived at this compromise, which was satisfactory if not ideal for the needs of all: the girl is to attend the smaller school for her first two years and will then transfer to the "better" one for the completion of her degree.

Limiting or narrowing your point of view is another way of discovering alternatives; by focusing in on an element of the problem you may find a better way to solve it. A woman I know had trouble in keeping herself outfitted decently, both as a financial and aesthetic matter. She couldn't afford to buy all the clothes she wanted, and she found that it was difficult for her to effectively match together many items she did buy. The color of the sweater (at home) just wouldn't allow for the blouse she had just bought to go with it; she made almost as many trips to return items as she did to purchase them. She thought about her problem and came up with the idea of buying and dressing only in blue or green, two colors that she felt were very flattering to her. This decision made her life much simpler. Now when she goes shopping she need worry only about style and fit for, whatever the shade of the blue or the green item, she is easily able to incorporate it into her existing wardrobe. And, of course, she has the possibility of many more possible combinations, making her seem—or at least feel—better dressed. This focusing in of her emphasis has made her life happier, and at the same time much easier.

A seeming detriment may be the alternative that can be used to your advantage. Here the procedure is similar to rejecting your present point of view in order to develop new alternatives; the difference is that you take the problem *itself* and reverse it so that it becomes, in effect, the viable solution. For example, Avis took its second-place position in the car rental market and came up with a slogan ("We try harder") that made this seeming inferiority into a good reason for the customer to do business with it rather than with its larger competitor. And remember madras? The colors kept running in the wash; understandably this made it somewhat difficult to sell the material until a bright-eyed genius thought of saying "Guaranteed to fade," thereby making the very real disadvantage into an apparent—and desirable—virtue: a genuine status symbol.

Or consider a woman I know who had the same feelings about wanting a child as the person I mentioned earlier; here, however, she was married, but unhappily. In such a situation most people would be very careful not to become pregnant, for it would seem that this would be an added complication. Not so for this woman. She recognized that one of the reasons why she married this man in the first place was her very strong desire for a child, and she realized that she would probably make the same error again because of her maternal desires. Therefore she fastened on the somewhat novel alternative of turning her dilemma to advantage: she decided to have the child by the man to whom she was still married. He was a perfectly acceptable father-type, as far as she was concerned, and she knew that by having the child by him she would not be inclined to hastily marry again because of her pressing need. Instead, she could then take the time to be sure that the next relationship was right for her. And, if she never really found a good one—well, at least she would have her child. She discussed her plan with her husband, and he agreed to this arrangement, as he too felt the same way about a child. And they both believed that they would be better parents than those who remained together while subjecting the child to their growing hostilities. This solution has worked out just as they expected; further, the woman is very happy today, living alone with her child, and quite selective about the men with whom she gets involved. By thinking creatively about her failing marriage, this woman was able to find in it a positive alternative for a major decision of her life.

As you see, there are a great many ways to find and determine most, if not all, of your options. Hopefully you have been testing them against the problem you set down earlier. If not, you now might want to go back over them and see what alternatives you can come up with in this specific regard. Be secure in the knowledge that there is a better way: an option that can do it for you. Of course, what's "better" is for a later chapter; for now just remember that you *can* find that gem. This security will give you a sense of freedom that in itself makes all your effort to discover it worthwhile.

For after all, freedom of choice is what this book is all about.

10

The Information You Need for Making a Good Decision

A famous if somewhat overworked line in vaudeville goes: "Don't confuse me with facts, because my mind's already made up." In real life, however, facts should never fluster one; they are invariably invaluable aids in making wise decisions. Confusion results not from the facts themselves, but rather from an inability to use them correctly and effectively. And the same is true of all our knowledge: properly used, knowledge can be priceless; use it badly and you're in trouble. Nor can you ever get too much information, or even enough. When you think of all those empty brain cells up there, just waiting to be filled, you know how little you *do* know.

Further, it happens that in our increasingly complex society this constant need for knowledge runs throughout the decision-making process. We had to know our goals, define our problems, and determine our options: all important pieces of information in themselves. Now, at this stage, the further knowledge we must seek is in amplification of something we already know: we have to learn more about each of these alternatives so that we can have a meaningful basis to evaluate them and then choose between them. This is true even if the decision is finally made intuitively with our right brain, rather than with the logical left, for the right brain too requires information. In addition, since we still want and need the reinforcement that the left brain will give us, we must be confident that it similarly knows all it has to so that our decisions are the best they can be. Therefore we should learn as much as we can about the problem before we have to decide on how to handle it, no matter which side of the brain we may use to make the decision, and even if we have a feeling (right brain) as to what we will probably do.

Specifically, we must now determine the advantages and disadvantages of each possibility, should it be chosen, and we ought to have some idea of the relative cost of the commitment. We have to recognize what our abilities and resources are, in terms of being able to successfully accomplish whichever of these options we decide to choose. And we have to realize what our obstacles in doing so may be. Most important of all: we certainly have to know how to find out what we want to know.

We are very fortunate in this regard: the brain is working all the time, almost automatically doing a large part of our research for us. It's like an investigative reporter, constantly asking who? what? why? when? where? and how? And it is continually receiving and absorbing a wealth of information of which we are generally unaware, and may not even care about at the time. This is knowledge of all kinds and qualities: facts, figures, feelings, biases, experiences, prejudices, history, fiction, and the like. All this information comes to us through our senses; we must see, hear, taste, touch, or smell it before the information can be transmitted to the brain.

Further, it is probable that we retain *all* these stimuli we are subjected to, possibly forever; certainly the brain seems able to remember things, even from the very distant past, when there is a purpose to do so. For example, a person under hypnosis can recall a license plate number, say, or a description, that to his conscious mind may have been forgotten or, at best, may be only a peripheral blur. By focusing in on the information under the prodding of the hypnotist, he makes it into a concrete, definable thing, thereby confirming that this knowledge was in his brain all the time. Similarly, under the probing of psychoanalysis, we can often retrieve some of those deeply buried memories of our earliest childhood. The sense of the distant past, the dim recognition of a place we think we were once at, the feeling of remembrance of a past event: all these signs of *déjà vu* are probably only some of these stored impressions, briefly surfacing in our conscious.

When we start thinking about a problem and its available alternatives, the right brain immediately and automatically summons up all the information it has ever collected that bears on this matter, and instantly you get its total instinctive and intuitive perception—and reaction. There is no delay, no hesitation; in fact, the impression—for that's all it is—is usually only momentary, and may even be gone as fast as it came. And this "gut feeling" or "hunch" or "sixth sense" should be valued and used; as Aeschylus said, "Memory is the mother of all wisdom."

Rarely, however, do we know everything; often there is more that must be specifically learned about our options. If this is the case, and provided that the problem is important enough to warrant this attention, the left brain comes into play. It seems to then logically sift through all the related stored-away impressions in both sides, consciously selecting those factors that it believes to be material and appropriate to the task at hand. The system resembles that of a computer bank; everything is celled away, just waiting for the proper buttons to be pushed in order to print it all out in detail.

With this material as background, we can then consciously seek out the additional information we need to fill the holes and plug the gaps and augment what we already have. And, hopefully, when we are ready to make our decision a number of these bits and pieces of information—both all that we have summoned up from the recesses of our brain and what we are now about to seek out—will coalesce to form an awareness that will be meaningful and will lead us to the right choice.

The question may fairly be asked: how much do you need to know? When do the few pieces of information—granted even their meaningfulness and importance—become enough? When can you feel confident in proceeding to the next steps of evaluating and choosing between these alternatives?

Unfortunately, although the question is clear, the answer is not. The best I can say is that it depends, and as a general rule you have to go it decision by decision. For example, I know a family that was about to buy a car; their choice of make and model was based primarily on the additional amount their loan payments would add to their monthly budget. The decision was arithmetical: they knew their financial limit and determined that the level of car they bought had to be within that figure. However, when these same parents were deciding on a college for their daughter, the tuition fee was barely considered; there were other, overriding concerns that caused them to virtually ignore the question of price and seek out information of a far more complex nature. And for us, as for them, each decision has its own needs, its own parameters; the amount of information that is crucial in one matter may not be sufficient in another.

Some people say you can never know too much, and of course that is true in a philosophical sense as well as the physical one of filling the brain. But then, we could probably spend the rest of our lives just collecting information, and we do—or should—have other things to attend to. Therefore, although we can never be sure that we have all the knowledge we would like, there must be a time when we do have enough: that is, sufficient for the purpose. As a practical matter there must be a limit to the amount of information we take the time to gather. Further, what is "enough" one day as the basis for a decision may not be the next. Foods and drugs sometimes go on the market after elaborate testing that presumably is sufficiently thorough to allow their use, only to be banned when a new piece of information develops. And if scientists in the labs, with their awesome array of instruments, can make this mistake of being satisfied too soon, understandably we mere mortals can have as great a difficulty when we are dealing with matters that can't be measured or tested or, at times, even felt or seen.

Obviously, more information is better than less, and this is especially true when your alternatives are very close in attractiveness. It is then that we would feel more comfortable with a larger amount of information, simply because there would be less insecurity for fear of overlooking an important element. Conversely, when the alternatives are not relatively equal in value or desirability, it becomes less necessary to be sure that all the information is in. However, no matter how much information you would like to have on each matter to be decided, you should always keep in mind the question of priorities that we discussed earlier: in your overall scheme of things, how much time is this decision worth? Remember that there is a limit on how much of yourself you can give to any one question, although we are obviously talking here of problems that are of some consequence and therefore need some attention. Even so, be careful that the time you devote to your decision—and the time collecting information pertinent to it—is not out of proportion to the matter itself.

Sometimes the essential, critical factor in what you decide may be one vital piece of information, or one seemingly insignificant act by another may do it. Remember the man with whom I was writing a book? When he told me that he was not in control of his actions, that was it: that one piece of information, with all its evident ramifications, was the catalyst for my decision to immediately terminate the relationship. In another situation, a man I know did not enter into an affair with a woman he had met and was turned on to, for he discovered that she was still married. Although this fact didn't seem to deter her, for him the possible complications now appeared substantial, with the pleasures considerably smaller by comparison. This catalytic bit of information tremendously modified his interest, and so he split. Or the one piece of vital information that ends the quest may be factual; the age requirement for an elective office, or the inflexible salary limits of a particular job, are cases in point. Therefore, do not be surprised if you suddenly know that *that's it*, and you don't need any more information. Decisions are often made this way, and when they are, consider yourself lucky that you didn't have to spend more time on these matters than you did.

But aside from the situation where one particular piece of information can be critical, rarely is there a fixed point at which anyone can really say, "Now I have all the information I need." Each matter is relative: how *much* you need to know is totally interrelated to *what* you need to know. Although these considerations are variable with each decision, in general they are fairly constant and consistent in their application, and can be easily used when necessary.

Before we get into the specifics of what you need to know, there are a few points I'd like to call to your attention. First, please realize that at this stage of making a decision I am talking about what is essentially close to, but not quite, *raw* information: not yet really appraised, but at the same time sufficiently evaluated so that you know it has some bearing on the question. As a simple matter of self-protection you have to be somewhat selective about the information you are merely gathering even before you get to the next step of fully evaluating it.

Not every piece of information is pertinent, or material. You want to know only that which will tell you something meaningful and relevant about the problem and its alternatives, and will be of some help in the final consideration of your options and your choice from among them. You must do a preliminary screening process as you collect your information: the nature and quality of the information you obtain on each of these is more important than its mere quantity. A multitude of insignificant details simply smother you and can lead to the confusion I mentioned earlier; it would be preferable to have fewer but salient pieces of information about the alternatives you are really considering. For example, if you are trying to decide about a job offer, the location of the firm may be of some importance to you, as it once was to me, whereas the floor the offices are on is obviously inconsequential and is a fact to be disregarded. (Unless, of course, you suffer from a fear of heights.) So, provided a detail has some relevancy, accept and hold it as basic information, to be evaluated later as part of the overall picture.

Also keep in mind that as you gather information, you may become aware of other alternatives that you might possibly have overlooked; of course you will add them to your list. You may even find that the problem is somewhat different than you envisaged it, or that a new problem is emerging; you must also utilize this information appropriately. Or you may deliberately begin to give less attention to some of your possible courses of action because you begin to realize, as you learn more about them, that they are not that interesting or exciting; therefore, you can now safely concentrate on the more promising ones. And, very important: remember that you may learn something that you are not too happy about, or may not even want to hear because it makes you uncomfortable. Don't avoid, or hide, or overlook such information. Often this knowledge is the most valuable of all.

Probably the first thing you'd like to know about each alternative is its possible outcome: what can its advantages be, if it turns out as successfully as you'd like it to? Understand that for now you need not evaluate the relative desirability of the various alternatives available to you; that comes later. What you should do now is to examine *each* of your options in an attempt to determine as best you can exactly what can positively happen if you should choose that one. What is its potential? What can this alternative achieve for you, assuming it is successful?

For example, a friend of mine had to choose between two jobs that he was offered at the same time. Upon investigation, he learned that one promised security, a regular working schedule, and a progressive rise to a well-paying level after a fairly long period of time. The other offered no security and was, in fact, a highly volatile situation; the opportunity to make a lot of money quickly by working exceedingly long hours was the compensating factor. So the possibilities were clear; he now knew what could happen with each of his alternatives. With this information he had the basis for a valid and meaningful choice. That's what I mean: you must know all the potential advantages of each option.

You also have to know what you stand to lose if the option you are considering does *not* work out. What are the risks? How serious, or how minor, may they be? What will the emotional damage be? And do you think you can handle it? Are there dangers involved? Is your decision irrevocable? Try to foresee what the consequences might be so that later you will not be surprised by the enormity of the outcome of the decision, should it fail.

You also need to know what the total cost of each alternative may be, and this involves several things. One is the price that you must pay (no matter how you are measuring this) in order to select and then act on each individual alternative. Will it be just time and energy? Or will it also be money and, if so, how much? What must you do? And for how long? Will this choice preclude or take you away from something else, in addition to having to forego the other alternatives?

And what about the emotional price? How much trauma, pain, anxiety, and insecurity are involved? Psychological cost is a strange and personal thing; mountains of material have been written about this and still no one .really understands it, beyond the recognition that such cost is a highly individual matter. Consequently there are no rules, or guidelines, or tools with which you can measure this cost; it is totally subjective. A doctor I know said it quite succinctly when he was explaining masochism to a class: "One person's pleasure is a lot of other people's pain. Only to different degrees." So the psychological cost is a factor only you can judge; the price can be an enormous one. Therefore you must try to clearly understand these emotional factors and the degree to which they will be involved. However, realize that these are usually right-brain feelings, so it may only be an instinct you have about this cost. But that may be all you need.

Then you must know if there is a continuing cost to which you will be committed after the decision is made. If so, what might this cost be? You've got to know, clearly and completely, all the ground rules that you will then be expected to play by as a result of making this choice. Often the decision itself is only the initiating factor for a number of consequences; it is important to remember always that the decision to choose a particular route also involves your future involvement with it as it unravels. The decision rarely, if ever, ends the matter; invariably the consequent demands upon you continue, and sometimes they do so even if you later want to change your mind about the commitment and end it. Take a marriage: it is staggering to realize what the laws of your state may forever demand of you, once you have bought the license and said the necessary words. Not even a divorce ends it cleanly all the time: children, joint financial ventures, co-ownership of a house or a car or art, even season football tickets—many ties can continue your involvement indefinitely.

Further, if several aspects of your life are affected by this alternative, you should try to get some idea of its tangential costs and consequences. How will this alternative interrelate with and concern you in areas that may go beyond the specific matter to be determined? Your job decision may affect others. I know a man who decided to turn down a promotion because it meant a move to another city; he was considering not only his own career, but also how it would affect his family. You must do the same appraisal as you try to determine what the possible price of each alternative may be.

All these cost factors are most important for you to know in your decision making. Often the alternative that, on first blush, seems most desirable will not be worth the price you have to pay—and it is better to have this information *before* you make your decision. Finding out afterward about some hidden costs might not be all fun and games.

Then, of course, you'd like information on how possible or probable it is for each of your alternatives to be successful if that should be the one you decide on. What factors are positive and in its favor, and what elements militate against it? How practical is it? Can it really be achieved? What is there about it that will make the decision a success, and what are the barriers or obstacles that might prevent you from achieving it? Or, to put it differently, what are its inherent pluses and minuses? What has each option got going for it that will help it happen, and what does it have about it that may be a problem? For example, a young television actress I know was trying to decide on whether she would be happier living in New York or Los Angeles. One bit of information helped in her final choice—statistics on the number of shows produced in each place. Similarly, it is vital for you to know, about each of your options, what are its real chances of making good if you should choose it.

In this regard, the matter of *you* is most important. You must have a clear and objective understanding of yourself—your knowledge, your abilities, your skills, your resources, and your attitudes. The Chinese philosopher Lao-Tse said, "He who knows others is clever; he who knows himself is enlightened." To attain this exalted state, you really should know how capable you are of achieving each particular alternative, and to know this you might first just consider your motivation. How do you feel about each of these alternatives? What are the inducements offered by these choices, and how intensely are you prompted to act on the individual options?

Obviously, if you don't have a strong desire to accomplish a particular alternative, your commitment will be correspondingly weak, and its consequent chances of success thereby reduced. Enthusiasm is worth a lot, and its power to accomplish an end should not be minimized. Therefore, you should try to determine your feelings about these alternatives; of course, since this is primarily right-brain awareness you probably already know this information. But it is also left-brain activity, especially when you think of this in the perspective of your goals. Either way, or both ways, try to determine the strength of your commitment.

Be careful, however, that you don't manufacture enthusiasm for any of your options; be honest with yourself about your feelings. Don't allow yourself to get carried away by hope, or expectation, or the desires of others; this is self-delusory and can only lead to trouble. For example, I know of a young boy who was sent by his parents—at some considerable financial sacrifice—to one of the "better" military academies so that he would become more of a man; he, poor soul, hates it and is desperate to quit. Yet he won't do this because he knows how much his graduation means to his parents, and he doesn't wish to live with the guilt of disappointing them. But to me, that's a shame; he is living his life for their reasons, not his. It really is important for you to evaluate your enthusiasm for each of your alternatives carefully. You must be aware of yourself.

As part of this awareness, you should know your abilities, and your skills. And you must know them objectively and realistically. You have to clearly see your limitations and your strengths, being wary of an inflated ego and equally cautious of self-deprecation; either one is self-defeating. To gain this awareness, you might ask yourself the following:

- What is needed of you to be able to achieve "success," and do you have these requisites?
- If it's a job that you are considering, does it require a specialized knowledge, or talent, or skill? And to what degree? (I can change the spark plugs on my car, but I'd starve as a mechanic.)
- Do you have the pertinent education and training?
- What about experience?
- Do you have the physical qualifications necessary, such as health and appearance?
- What about your emotional makeup?
- Are patience and tolerance required? Do you have sufficient of these?
- Will conformity be required? If so, how willing and able are you to fit the mold?
- Do you get along with certain people better than others (as does the hairdresser I told you about)?
- What about your emotional needs?
- If you feel anger, can you live with restraint should the alternative you are considering prohibit the full expression of it?
- Will it be frustrating and debilitating, or can you accept it?
- Can you accept the trauma of possibly being fired, if you should take the more speculative job?
- How fragile are your feelings? How strong are your defenses?
- What about the emotional needs of the people with whom you are involved, and to whom you owe a responsibility?
- How do you think they will react to each alternative?
- What about your resources: the friends who can help, the contacts you may have, the money you may need?
- Finally, how do you *feel* about this position, or this opportunity?

The same kind of questions must be asked about the other person, or persons, involved in the situation. There are things you should want to know about a relationship, say, whether it is with a business associate or a bed partner. These involve questions you have to ask yourself: that is, what do *you* think are the answers to these questions? How do *you* see him?

- What are his (or, of course, her) values?
- His strengths?
- His weaknesses?
- Does he share some, or many, of your interests?
- Does he have the same kind of sense of humor you do? (I consider this a "biggie.")
- Do you enjoy being with him?
- Do you look forward to seeing him?
- Do you have fun with him?
- Or does he bore you? (If so, sometimes or a lot?)
- What is his self-image?
- What do you think his image is of you?
- What are the things you like about the person?
- What are the qualities you don't like?
- And what are the things you absolutely can't stand?
- What is his intelligence/intellectual level, vis-à-vis yours?
- What about physical activities (like sex, if it's that kind of relationship)?
- What's his emotional level?
- Is he gentle?
- Kind?
- Loving?
- Exciting?
- Patient?
- Compliant?
- Strong?
- Romantic?
- Quiet?
- Understanding?
- Possessive?
- Staid?

- Moody?
- Sophisticated?
- Do you get along politically?
- Religiously?
- Morally?
- Is he communicative?
- Does he smoke? (This is a big one for some people, even more than "does he drink?")
- How important are material things to him?
- Is he conventional?
- *Too* conventional?
- Rich?
- Rich enough?
- Ambitious?
- Cheap?
- Sensitive?
- Decisive?
- Neat?
- Tolerant?
- Curious?
- Inquisitive?
- Is he honest?
- Open?
- Truthful?
- Do you respect him?
- Finally, is he worth your vulnerability?

Many things to find out, much information to gather. Obviously, not everything I suggest is pertinent in every situation; each has its own specifics. Clearly, you have to use these factors selectively, embracing only those that are relevant to you, and expanding, modifying, or adding to them if it is necessary or helpful. And always keep this in mind: if your collection of this information isn't honest, it's you who will pay the price.

11

Getting Your Information

Now then, how do you get the information you need? Where do you find it?

Your first move is to put your inner computer to work. You should try to summon up and marshal whatever information your brain already contains about each of the alternatives you are considering. A little concentration and intensive thought may give you unexpected rewards; it is always surprising to discover how much we already know about so many things. Dredge it all up; keep it handy.

Then, with an eye to the specifics of what you want to learn about your option, you must begin to ask questions. And the first person to do this with is yourself: I've gone over a wide range of

143

information that you can learn about the situation simply by asking yourself the pertinent questions. That, in itself, may be enough.

Then, of course, you have the person—or persons—with whom you are involved. If you are focusing on a potential relationship, obviously you have been doing a lot of talking. If you are considering a job possibility, you should do as much interviewing as being interviewed. Whatever the situation, the people with whom you will be directly involved are probably your best source; you need only to extract—subtly and politely—the information you need.

You may also have to make pertinent inquiries of people who conceivably are in a good position to give you helpful answers; this, of course, depends on what you are deciding. Different people have different talents; you simply have to match up the right person with the right questions to get what you need. Take the matter of buying a house and wanting to be sure of its desirability. Obviously such an evaluation would be within the range of an architect, who probably can give you some excellent information and advice; far better, certainly, than even a smart lawyer. A carpenter or, better, a contractor, would also probably be of value here; the particular matter is obviously within their expertise.

But no way would you ask any of these professionals for their opinions on your latest amour; that would be ludicrous. However, your family and friends who know you well can all give you good advice on both these subjects: they know your tastes and your needs, and enough about you to add valuable insight and information to the mix. They obviously are people you can trust and consult on virtually any of your problems; they are your old standbys.

Then, as the occasion warrants, there are teachers, clergymen, business acquaintances, others who work for a firm you are considering joining, school advisers of all kinds (if you're still a student). Every one of these is a valuable source of information on certain matters; usually in order to get it you need only ask. As a last—but very competent—resort, there are professional people in all fields: doctors, lawyers, accountants, whatever; good people all, but usually wanting to be recompensed for the use of their brain. And certainly, at times, you should gladly pay for what you want to know. At least, that's what I tell my clients if they complain about my bill. . . . Not incidentally, however, one of the best—and free—professionals available is a librarian. I am in awe of the amount of knowledge these people have, especially in terms of where to find necessary and valuable information on virtually any subject. And you'll find that most of them love to be asked!

You also have to ask the right questions—and that, I can tell you, is really a science. But it's also a little like a *Life* magazine photographer I knew: he once told me that even for the simplest assignment, one that probably would use at most three pictures on one page, he easily shot more than a thousand negatives. By doing this, he said, there was no way that he could fail to get the photos needed. In the same manner, if you ask enough questions, you are bound to get some valuable answers. Just don't be afraid or hesitant to continue asking, even if you think your questions may be considered dumb. The more you ask, the more you will be told; sometimes you can get a lucky break and be given information that never occurred to you to even look for. People can always say they're sorry, and refuse to answer; however, as far as you're concerned, the more you venture, almost certainly the more you will gain. For it is absolutely incredible how much people will tell you, if you will only ask—and keep asking, even ridiculous things. Dick Cavett suggests this; he tells the story of an interview he once had with Bette Davis, who complimented him on the fact that she found him easy to talk to because he never asked embarrassing questions. To which Cavett, ever eager to entertain, audaciously asked: "Okay, then, tell me how you lost your virginity?" This, of course, got a howl of laughter from his audience, but more interestingly it also got an honest answer from her.

The same is true even of strangers; everyone wants to get into the act and show how much he knows. I once did a considerable amount of real estate work for a client who specialized in small shopping centers. By spending a day, wandering from store to store and just chatting with the merchants I met, I got more valuable information about the operation than a battery of accountants, working a week, were able to give him; all of it gained simply by asking simple questions. Of course, it would be best if these questions are oriented to your goals; certainly they should at least be directed to obtaining information about the decision you have to make. But even seemingly dumb questions get answers that, for the most part, are good ones. People love to talk, and talk, and talk. Just give them the opportunity—ask!

Sometimes you can get information simply by being curious. A man I know happened to stumble on a new alternative (and the ultimate solution to his problem) in exactly this way. He had been thinking about going back to school for some advanced study he wanted, but didn't know how he could fit it into his schedule, what with a family and a job to contend with. One morning, as he was waiting for his train (he commutes to work from Long Island to New York City), he noticed a group of men at one end of the platform, all carrying textbooks. He wondered what was going on, so he walked over to ask. What do you know: Adelphi University, through its School of Business Administration, was giving courses on the morning run to the city, which would eventually lead to a master's degree in business administration! Here was the answer to my friend's problem, discovered only because he was curious—and not embarrassed to ask.

You can even, in a sense, "ask" information of written material; you simply have to know what to look for in order to get your answers. For example, I wanted to go on vacation to a particular Caribbean island about which I could not get any trustworthy firsthand information; none of my friends or acquaintances had been there. But I did get (from the government tourist office) a number of brochures about the various hotels on the island; these, not surprisingly, contain a wealth of information. Brochures, of course, are obviously blatant advertising ploys, and should be treated somewhat as you treat a salesman. Unquestionably, they have but one aim: your money. And, of course, they are biased. But, taking this into consideration, you *can* get a lot of information from such material that can help you make a better decision as to where to go. And brochures even have one advantage over salesmen: they are *written*, so later you can't be told that "you misunderstood" and no one ever said such a thing.

In this case, the style of the brochure is the first thing to look for. Remember that this material represents the hotel's own self-image:

this is not only the picture they want you to get, it is also their own impression of what they are (or, at least, of what they'd like to be). For example, I have seen one that has not only a Botticelli reproduction on its parchment cover, it also has another from Michelangelo on the underlying cardboard second cover! Before I even opened that brochure, I knew a lot about the place, which was confirmed when I saw both their rates and the aerial view of their grounds. This is a resort that smacks of wealth and high society; it also means all kinds of indulgent pampering in return for high tips. It is a far cry from the other end of the spectrum: a single photo-offset page that guarantees "a quiet, old-fashioned place to rest and relax." Which, of course, means they have very little in the way of facilities if, in fact, they have any. And there's probably a close resemblance to the old mom and pop candy store: not too many on the staff. Then, somewhere in between, is a very simple folder with several pages slipped in; this one offers "plenty of room to be yourself"; you know that it is not fancy, not formal, and not nearly as expensive as the Roman Empire you first looked at. Now, with all this basic information—that is, the style and price of the place—you can easily pick out from your bunch of brochures those that initially appeal and those that don't. In fact, you probably had some intuitive feelings about each of these as you removed them from the envelopes, and have already in effect done this.

Then look carefully at the pictures of the resorts you have narrowed your choice down to; they'll tell you a lot more. Here you not only can get an idea of their self-image, but you can get some clues as to what their *best* is. Remember, that's what they're showing you: their ultimate. They certainly are not going to put forth their lesser side, so you know that what you see is the cream of what they have to offer. Therefore, you can now compare their best against that of the others you are considering. For example, what's the age range of the guests? Are they old, rundown, dreary-looking, therefore assuring a staid, very quiet week? Or are they younger week-ender types? (One brochure takes no chances: it shows guests from seventeen to seventy, all laughing and carousing together; you know that's a fake.) And what does the dining-room dress look like? Pictures of waiters in black tie at island resorts mean mink is *de riguer;* that always turns me off but, obviously, some people like this. Conversely, will you be comfortable in jeans (if you wear them)? Then there's always the picture of a "typical" bedroom. Is it simple or fancy? Does it look cold and formal, or is it warm and inviting, and conducive to your frame of mind and your own self-image?

Finally, what are their facilities like? For example, when you see a picture of a corner of *a* tennis court, and no mention of others, you know there is only one—which may or may not be of consequence to you. On the other hand, there's one place—I swear this is true—that has *eighteen* tennis courts, an eighteen-hole golf course, sunfish, scuba, snorkeling, crab races, casino, boutiques, babysitters (*that* says something about the crowd), and a branch of the Chase Manhattan Bank! It also has bars all over the place: there's a pool bar, two beach bars, bars in the five restaurants, certainly several in the casino and the disco, and even a 19th Hole bar at the golf course. You don't have to stumble very far for the next one; of course, if you're not much of a drinker, you might have to keep stepping over fallen bodies. But fear not: they also have "a fully staffed medical clinic." Without a doubt, this brochure gives you sufficient information. Or warning.

So, even as with these advertisements, there *are* ways of getting information; it all boils down to the art of inquiry, for with it you can get just about everything you need to know to come to a wise decision. You simply have to get in the habit of asking, and then asking some more. Look for specifics; go for the facts. You are, after all, spending *your* time and money.

However, there is an aspect of investigation that is vital: you must also listen. Listening is extremely difficult—and also uncommon. Most people don't listen; they're too busy talking to themselves. Or they're too concerned with what they are doing, or thinking, or just about to do. Listening is hard work; it requires effort, and concentration, and energy, and all are in short supply in our society.

Listening to what someone is telling you requires, in a sense, that you care about him and want to know what he has to say. I once worked for a man who I was sure never listened, or cared; one morning, when I arrived at the office, he greeted me with his perfunctory "How are you?" I tested him. "Terrible," I said, "my car was stolen and my wife has left me." "That's nice," he muttered, as he continued about his affairs.

Even worse is the person who is merely waiting to interject his own comments the instant you take a breath, thereby interrupting your pearls of wisdom. We all know too many of such folk, and how you deal with them is your own affair. But if you want to gather information and gain knowledge, you've got to learn to listen. Of course, this assumes that the person who is speaking has something of value to say to you. If he doesn't, why are you talking to him in the first place? So you've got to pay attention to what he says. You've got to concentrate on what is being told you so that you can understand and comprehend it for your own future use. I know so many people who just talk *at*—not *to*—each other; they don't respect the other or their relationship because they no longer have the slightest idea what either is about. But you really can't know what the other person is thinking or feeling, unless you ask—and listen.

This does not mean that you should listen to, and focus in on, everything that's said to you; an important aspect of concentration is the ability to listen selectively. You must listen carefully enough to extract the essence, or theme, or point of what is being said. The coloration and explanatory material surrounding it may or may not be valuable, and can be used or discarded like so much window dressing if it is not of consequence. You must be like the impressionistic painter who selects from the wealth of images presented to him at any given moment only those few that are of meaning to him, and then puts his full concentration into these. But first you must hear, as he must see, the totality of what is being communicated in order to make this determination of what is important.

Sometimes a person says a great deal without ever getting to his point; it is then that you must mentally supply the emphasis for him and clarify his idea in your own thought processes (not, of course, interrupting him to display your wisdom). And this can be especially so if he is deliberately withholding information. Therefore you must listen with your inner, or third, ear; the ability to hear what has *not* been said can be most valuable. And it is very hard to cultivate. But it is immensely worth the effort to develop it, for I believe that more valuable information is hidden away and not conveyed than is often expressed.

Further, you must be careful that you are cognizant of what *should* be said, and then you can be more aware of its absence when it is not expressed—especially if it's something you want to hear. For example, a couple I know had what seemed to be a developing relationship, and soon she began to seriously talk about the possibility of living together. During one particularly heavy discussion, the woman offered many good reasons why she wanted to move in; she talked about how good he was to her and what he did for her. But the one vital thing she never said was that her compelling reason for cohabitation was her love for him and her desire to share with him; never a word as to what she could do for him and what she was willing to give to the relationship. The man was listening for these crucial words; their absence scared him sufficiently so that he not only refused to present her with his key but he also quickly found other companions less introspective and less taking of his attentions.

So listen selectively and attentively; hear what the other person says, and hear too what he doesn't say but really means. You can thereby save yourself much later anguish.

You must also be aware of the meanings of words. You need to clearly understand what the speaker is saying, and in the context in which he means it. Sometimes people use words in other than their dictionary meanings, and sometimes the words they use are not even colloquially correct. You must learn to interpret what is being said so that at least you can comprehend the information being imparted. For example, at a recent government hearing, an agency head who was testifying was asked what happened to the porpoises that are caught in tuna fishermen's nets and subsequently die when the nets are raised aboard the boats. "They are returned to the ecosystem," he said.

"Is that the government's way of saying they are thrown overboard?" asked one of the questioners.

"Yes," said the official, reluctantly.

Or take the word "indicate." This is one of the loosest and most abused words in our language, and I for one am never quite sure what is meant when I hear it. When a person says, "He indicated to me that he didn't want to do it . . . ," what is he saying? The most common dictionary definitions of the word are that it is (a) a sign of something (such as hesitation indicating unwillingness); or (b) that something is pointed out or pointed to (as a place on a map); or (c) something is stated or expressed briefly and in a general way (as to indicate one's intentions). Well, did the man who "indicated" he didn't want to do this thing merely shrug his shoulders; or did he point to the door, suggesting that the person telling us the story should leave; or did he say, "I don't want to do it"? One is not sure, and since it is conceivable that the first two actions may have been misinterpreted, you must ask again to focus in on and narrow down the speaker's statement.

Sometimes words are used loosely to escape from being pinned down to specifics. Often this is an easy way out of a situation because everyone thinks they're satisfied—at least for a while. For example, a friend of mine was not too happy with her job, for she is bright enough to have quickly outgrown it; she had been pressing the firm she works for to give her a promotion to a better, more interesting, and more challenging one. She had been told that they "loved" her, and they would soon do something. Just "be patient," she was told. That approach is understandable, to a point, but no one had said what she really wanted to know: for how long was she to be patient? And for *what*? When she finally posed these questions, she discovered the painful truth: her employers didn't know. However, when confronted with these pertinent issues, they too gave it some thought, and now she has a position in which she's very happy. But if she hadn't forced management to think about specifics, she would probably still be in the original situation, being very impatient. And unhappy.

Further, your listening should be not only to words; you must also learn to listen to *how* the words are said—you must observe both the tone and the attitude of the speaker. You may find this information helpful when you have to judge the relative value of what you heard, and so you should be aware of it.

You should also "listen" to what the person does; you've heard the truism that actions speak louder than words. Hear the behavior patterns; you can learn a lot. This can be especially true in the area of relationships, where your alternatives are more emotional in nature and your outside sources of information are few—if any. Here you really have to depend on what you learn from the other person. And in such a situation, what people do can often be more revealing than what they say. The person who is disrespectful of others will be disrespectful of you; the person who breaches other people's confidences or lies to them will do the same to you—no matter what he says. (Many white-collar crooks are caught only because they trusted another crook who, once the going got tough, turned on his partner in order to save his own neck. A crook *is*, after all, a crook.) And the person who is considerate of the feelings of others will be careful of yours. Conversely, the man who is never on time for a date is telling you something; so is the one who habitually doesn't call when he says he will, because he was "busy." You really have to look at all the signs for every bit of information you can get. Communication is too often the hardest art of all, and must be augmented in every way you can.

Finally, I'd like to give you one last tip, one known by every trial lawyer in the business, especially the good ones. These are men singularly adept at this technique of asking and listening that I have been talking about, and they do it better than almost anyone else around. But they add to it; they have made it into an art by going just the one step further—they ask *again*, based on what they have just been told, and in particular *what they heard*, either verbally or visually. Earlier I said you must keep questioning and questioning; this was a somewhat simplistic statement of what I am referring to. You do keep asking questions, but you must ask very direct and pointed ones. You zero in on the information you have just received. By carefully listening to the reply you have been given, you know what to ask next. One answer leads, inexorably, to the following more pertinent question. And on and on, till you get through the nonsense and to the stuff that really makes sense.

If you start, however, with a set idea, or a fixed list of questions, you find yourself in the position of waiting only for the pause after the reply to get on to the next inquiry, and without listening to the

response just given. One of the Sunday night television inter-
viewers is invariably guilty of precisely this: he has a clipboard of
questions, and his job seems to be to get through an hour and a
half by having asked them all. Unfortunately, he leaves his guest
somewhat baffled and his audience frustrated. An exchange goes
something like this: Guest: "But when I opened the box I was
shocked at what I found inside." Host: "And what is your favorite
color?" This is what is known as a non sequitur and, although
such situations may be considered funny in shaggy dog stories,
they have no place in your search for information. You must follow wherever the search may lead; you must listen attentively and
selectively to what is being said, and to what may not have been
said but *should* have been said, and you must use this as the basis
for your next penetrating and incisive question.

However, don't become so involved on this chase that you
forget to ask what you must know. A list of questions—such as the
one I suggested earlier—that help remind you of the areas or
points on which you want information can be very helpful, and
should be used so that you don't neglect asking them at the appropriate time. For example, a friend of mine was becoming involved with a man who was also becoming involved with her. But
the two of them were constantly talking about whether or not they
wanted this relationship, and what it meant to them. They were
both so compulsive about this subject that they never dropped it
long enough to find out if they could communicate or enjoy each
other on any other level. Finally this "relationship" bogged down
in its own quicksand, and of its own weight. Had my friend asked
these other important questions, she might have discovered that
there was nothing more. And she probably would have learned it
earlier, thereby saving herself some time and emotional energy.

In sum, you must always ask in order to know, and you must
listen in order to understand. Further, at this stage you need not
determine the value of the information or the extent to which you
agree with it; at this point all you want to do is to gather and
comprehend what is being said. You should be impartial and
objective in collecting information, like a big vacuum cleaner
sucking in everything. Later on, when you evaluate it all, you can

be very subjective. But now, just play prosecuting attorney. Collect all the information you can, for you need all the edges you can get. Be determined to find out the whole truth, whatever it may be. Above all, be responsive to what you hear—whether aurally or with the inner ear. Make your questions, and your questioning, into an art. The decision you save by means of a vital piece of information may be your own.

12

How to Evaluate Your Information

When I go into court to try a case, I am governed by certain rules of evidence and procedure. These have developed over the centuries and serve a simple purpose: they are an attempt to ensure that the truth will out. The judge and the jury need as much help as they can get in the trial of a case and in fairly deciding its outcome, and it is precisely for this reason that these elaborate rules are in practice. And since it seems to me that some of these tools can be exceedingly helpful to you in making your daily decisions, I'm going to talk about several of them so that you too can profit by their use.

At the heart of all the guidelines built into our courtroom procedure is the simple matter of evaluation—the examination and judgment of the quality and worth of the evidence. This is crucial in a trial, where the trier of the case must decide precisely what occurred and how it came about. Time is irreversible, every situation is unique, and memories are faulty; therefore the scales of justice are not always perfect. The best a jury can do is try to come as close to the truth as reasonably possible: "It seems that this is *probably* what happened...." Consequently, the evidence must be weighed with the utmost care; poor judgment in this regard can unquestionably result in bad decisions.

Similarly, you must do the same—only in your case, the decision is going to be a prediction (and a hope) of what *will* probably happen. Once you evaluate the information in your possession with all the deliberation it deserves, you will make a choice that you want to see succeed. Therefore, the better able you are to judge the quality and worth of your information, the better are your chances of success. And here the old cliché is very true: quality, not quantity, is what counts.

In general, this matter of evaluation is one in which you must examine *everything* that has any bearing on the problem—information about yourself, your situation, your options, your goals. All this enters into the decision-making process, and all of it counts. Therefore, it should all be systematically examined. You must be logical, ordered, and above all questioning and analytical, like a lawyer in court.

Essentially you should look for two elements as you evaluate all this material. First, you want to know the validity of the material. How good is it? Is it honest, accurate, and reliable? Can you depend on its truthfulness and completeness? Can you fully trust it? Second, and *only* if you are satisfied as to the first, you want to know the extent of its meaning and worth. Of course, it had to have some apparent value, or there would have been no point in even being concerned at all about its validity. But the question now becomes *how* meaningful is it? How much value does it have? What is its importance?

I am not suggesting that you should want to check the validity of your information because people generally lie; and it is not necessarily because I believe that you may have been deliberately told an untruth. But in court I often find that there is more to the story than is told at first blush; the witness is "amazed" at the suggestion that what he left out is "that important." Nor am I too surprised at the "small" exaggerations and colorations that sometimes and somehow creep into the narrative. Obviously, I am not alone in this morass of half-truths and incomplete stories, and consequently our system has developed some protective measures. They are simply a way to find the truth, or as much of it as possible, and not be misled by information that may be superficially convincing but that in actuality has little validity. Further, if in fact a deliberate lie *was* told, these methods will help to discover this too.

Probably the most potent weapon in this fight for sanity is cross-examination—that is, the piercing scrutiny of the witness by the adverse party. One of our foremost treatise writers on evidence, Dean Wigmore, says that cross-examination is "beyond any doubt the greatest legal engine ever invented for the discovery of truth." And although I, and every lawyer with whom I've ever discussed this, fully agree on its value, it is interesting to note that cross-examination is found primarily in the English system and our own, but not on the Continent. There, in the interest of economy and because of a difference in the way justice is administered, the witnesses are essentially questioned by an examining judge. However, in our system the cross-examination of adverse witnesses is a matter of right in every trial of a disputed issue of fact.

Good cross-examination tests for many things; it is a subject that literally fills shelves in the law libraries. I am going to touch on it here only in some of its more important aspects and will not trouble you with the qualifications and abstruse nuances lawyers sometimes get so worked up about. Also, realize that at any given time only some of these points will be pertinent; however, I promise you that all will have their value and their day in (your) court.

As I sit at the bar during a trial, listening to a witness recount his tale, I am constantly thinking: Does he make sense? Do I believe him? I do not mean that I actively distrust him, but I constantly maintain a healthy skepticism. I wonder: Is he telling us something he actually believes? How sincere does he seem? Even if he seems to be trustworthy, how possible—and plausible—is his story under the circumstances? I have heard witnesses claim to have seen things under light, weather, or distance conditions where they were patently not possible to perceive. For example, a woman I know almost split up with her fiancé because her cousin was "sure" she had seen him at a disco with another woman. When my friend went to this club to verify the possibility that this had happened, she realized that under the circumstances what her cousin described was not at all credible. There just wasn't enough light across the dance floor to identify anyone, as this woman was claiming to do. Furthermore, out of vanity, the woman hadn't even been wearing her glasses—a "minor" fact we found out later!

Then there is the matter of the witness's memory: how good is it? Though, as I said earlier when talking about the brain, we are *capable* of virtually total recall, it is very rare to see it happen. That's why John Dean, whatever you may think of his morals, was such a mental marvel. On a conscious level, at least, people *do* seem to forget with the passage of time. And so you wonder: Are you being told of experiences this man actually had? Or is he deceiving himself—and possibly us—in thinking he remembers something that didn't happen? People are suggestible, and sometimes a story they have only heard takes on the trappings of reality for them. Sometimes, possibly because it gives them a sense of importance, they enlarge or improve upon a tale, inventing items that give it more significance or meaning than it had, or that change its whole coloration. Therefore you must be careful of stories that are too complete or too perfect; too often they are also not too true.

Conversely, there is the problem of stories that are incomplete simply because of faulty preparation or investigation. I liken this to reading yesterday's newspaper—that is, depending on information that is now outdated. Conditions change rapidly; today's news is already tomorrow's history. And so you have to be sure that what you're getting is recent, up-to-the-minute information; anything less can be misleading and even counter-productive. In a trial I observed, for example, an attorney made an extensive analysis of another case, going to great pains to show its resemblance to the one in which he was engaged. He was brilliant in

his argument, for he believed that if the jury accepted this similarity, they would also have to go along with its conclusion,
which obviously favored him. Unfortunately, his opponent had
done his homework and knew one thing this man did not: that
this other case had been reversed on appeal! So in effect the first
man dug his own grave, and very well at that.

You must be careful that you do not allow something of this sort
to happen to you as you use information in making your decisions. You've got to be certain, especially if the information is
important enough, that it is still valid and accurate. You've got to
check copyright dates in books you depend on. You've got to find
out (subtly, of course) if the doctor who recommends an operation
knows of the latest drugs. You've got to be sure that you're dealing
with the most recent and updated information you can get.

I have also mentioned that memories are often faulty; it sometimes can be very difficult to get even an approximation of the
whole truth. It may be that the witness is honestly unable to remember because so much time has gone by, but it can especially
happen when he has a personal interest of some kind in the outcome of the case and conveniently "forgets." This matter of bias is
called "competency"; in earlier times such witnesses were totally
disqualified as being "incompetent." But now the law has
broadened so as to allow virtually anyone to testify, no matter how
great his involvement, provided he is physically capable of observation and communication. Of course, the weight that is given to
his evidence is for the jury to determine. I have seen cases where
this prejudice has been shown on cross-examination to be so intense that it actually worked in reverse and against the party
propounding the testimony.

Prejudice is a strange phenomenon: we all have it, and we also
all use it; yet most of us deplore it. Prejudice is a preconceived
opinion, generally formed without knowledge or any careful
thought. Almost invariably it is a programmed reaction the individual is totally unaware of that colors information in subtle and
even devious ways. It is present in all of us to a greater or lesser
degree; no one is immune. Lawyers play with it all the time: they
pick jurors on the basis of their supposed prejudices, and they try
to introduce evidence in such a way as to trade upon these

predilictions. And, of course, witnesses will inadvertently be influenced in their narratives by their own preconceptions, which no one may be aware of.

The biggest danger with prejudice is that it is very difficult and at times impossible to detect, even by the most adroit questioning. Sometimes the best an attorney can do in court is to suggest its presence and hope that the jurors will recognize its presence in another. The paradox is that people can never see their own bias, but very often can easily smell it in another. And, in the matter of making your decisions, you probably have to do the same: trust your right brain to do this for you, so that you get as complete and unprejudiced a picture as possible.

Another way to test for prejudice or inaccurate information is by corroboration. How does the story you are being told measure up against the other material you already have? Is it consistent and of a piece, or does it seem to be at odds with other facts you have learned? Of course, if there is corroboration by previously learned information, this may enhance its value, although this is not necessarily so; both sources may be wrong. If, on the other hand, there seems to be an inconsistency between two pieces of infor- mation, you certainly should approach both with extra caution.

But the worst to deal with when you are seeking accurate in- formation is the person who deliberately lies. Whatever his reason—self-interest, ego to the point of dangerous braggadocio, or simply a pathological imbalance—such a person can cause a great deal of harm. And, because his behavior is calculated and intended, such lies are extremely hard to discern. This person's story is usually quite rational and consistent; the standard test of "does it make sense?" is usually met; and his demeanor is of the utmost sincerity. So you may be in trouble if someone like this is in your life; here, of course, there are no obvious cautionary warnings and therefore the lie is difficult to cope with. However, if you have the slightest suspicion (probably right brain) that the person is being untruthful, you must be especially concerned with corroboration of the information he offers—particularly if it is important in making your decision. Check back in your memory for previous experiences, if any, you may have had with him. Ask others about his reputation for veracity and dependability. See if this information he is offering is consistent with previous statements he may have made. And, of course, if you discover that he has in fact lied to you, having his fingernails pulled out, one by one, with a pair of pliers, would seem perfectly justified. Vengeance is sweet.

This need for cross-examination to determine truth is the reason for one of the most important of the exclusionary rules of evidence: the hearsay rule. Simply put, hearsay is testimony about something that is not based on the witness's own personal knowledge or observation but rather on what someone else said. And unless this evidence falls within certain very specific exceptions, it is always excluded. The reason is obvious: since the statements of the third party that are only being reported cannot be subjected to cross-examination in order to test their validity, there is no fair way to be sure that the facts they. purport to convey are true; therefore, they must be disallowed.

For example, in the situation I just described, the testimony might be: "My cousin told me that she saw my fiancé out dancing with another woman." Now, although it is probably true that the cousin did say this to the person telling us the story, the question of whether or not the fiancé *was* dancing with another woman is pure hearsay and, in a court of law, would be excluded. Although there may be no dispute as to the *words* having been said by the cousin, there can be a very important question for the jury to determine as to the supposed *facts* of her statement. Unless she herself can be cross-examined about the statement to determine its truth and accuracy, it cannot be allowed in as evidence to show that the fiancé *was* out dancing with another woman. This repetition of her statement by another person is hearsay and therefore is not allowed as proof of the event. Certainly, too, there is always the possibility that the cousin did *not* quite say this, but that the statement itself is being misquoted—which is all the more reason to exclude it. At least in court. As for you, be particularly cautious when you depend on any hearsay evidence.

My point, I think, is clear. You must question and doubt. You must wonder and analyze and constantly assure yourself that the information you are dealing with is valid; that, in fact, it does make sense. You must be confident that it is honest and plausible and factual before you attempt to use it. In this regard you may recall that earlier I spoke of trust and the unfortunate lack of it in our society, and I do not mean to reduce this in value even further. Rather, I am suggesting that once you have properly evaluated the person, or the information that he has conveyed to you, and you come up with positive marks in this regard, you can then trust with even more confidence. Blind, unquestioning trust creates problems; well-founded, dependable trust does not. And this is true no matter what area of life your decision may be in: whether it be in your relationships, your career, your social life, or your creative endeavors.

You must also be careful that you yourself do not contribute to any inaccuracies of information. There are several ways in which you might do this. Probably the biggest danger in this regard is the matter of assumptions. Assumptions suppose that a thing is true, tnat it can be accepted at face value, and that it need not be verified or questioned. Most often an assumption is based on the naive belief that it has "always" been so. That's generally the tipoff: anyone who says "I've always known it to be true that . . ." is probably still living in the Stone Age, where he learned what he claims to know. That information—because it so possibly can be misleading—is usually worse than useless. To do something because it has "always" been done this way can even be dangerous; I really wish that word could be barred from our language. You should *always* remember that those who unquestioningly accept and repeat the past probably haven't learned from it; they will just continue making the same bad decisions, probably always.

Further, this repetition of history's yesterday simply because it presumably should be revered, and therefore not questioned, may even be an easy way to manipulatively perpetuate a great deal of misinformation or at least hinder a clear understanding of the pertinent information. For example, take the traditional myth of the sanctity of marriage. This relic, which is responsible for having made millions of people feel guilty for wanting or participating in a divorce, is presumably interpreted from the Scriptures and therefore is sometimes treated like pure gospel. But the fact is that the marriage vow, with monogamy and fidelity as its basis till death do us part, didn't become firmly imposed on or sacramental in our society until the fourth century. So it hasn't "always" been so; it has only been this way for a mere pittance of time in man's history. Nor, of course, is indissolubility the rule even today in the majority of the cultures of our world. And, finally, you should know that when this concept of the permanence of marriage did become dogma, the average life expectancy was not much more than thirty! The complexion of the matter changes a bit when you have this additional information, doesn't it?

Assumptions can also color your evaluation of your options. You may be following a pattern of behavior based on the premise that you know what someone else is thinking, or will do, and you define your alternatives accordingly. But it is difficult enough to know what we *ourselves* are thinking; to believe that we can get into another person's mind and determine *their* thoughts is presumptiveness of the worst order. These assumptions of another's behavior are often so patently false that you would be wise not only to ignore them immediately when they come to mind, but even to consider acting in direct opposition to them. They are in general based on our own insecurities: our own fears of failure, or rejection, or disapproval. Too rarely do they have a basis in fact. For example, a charming woman I know has recently gone through a divorce and is understandably feeling great pangs of loneliness. There are nights when she desperately would like to talk or be with someone, simply to assuage the suffocating depression she feels, but she assumes that her friends are either too busy or too bored to comfort her, and she is afraid of alienating them further. The presumed rejection simply adds to her growing feeling of desolation. But of course she has done this to herself by not allowing the alternative of making the call and asking for help. If she did, she just might be pleasantly surprised. And entertained.

Therefore, if you have been assuming *anything*, or finding yourself or people you have been dealing with using phrases like "of course this is so" or "I'm sure of it" or "it's always been this way," you had better proceed with great caution and examine what is told you as "fact" very carefully. Learn to question everything. Accept nothing unless it can be shown to be so. Some assumptions *are* true, of course; as Henry Kissinger once said in response to being accused of paranoia, "Even paranoids have enemies." Accordingly, you must analyze statements and beliefs and information with cynicism and skepticism, constantly asking yourself if your information makes sense *now*. And, if it does, accept and use it; if not, dump it.

Manipulative use of language is another danger to watch out for when you are evaluating the validity of your information. In the last chapter I talked a little about communication, and the care required in its use; you must be even more wary of its calculated misuse. Sometimes people deliberately imply something that is not true; they intend that you make the wrong assumptions and thereby infer what they want you to believe. In effect, they are trading on your belief in their sincerity. And, by doing it this way, they are not guilty of an out-and-out lie; at most they will admit to a "simple misunderstanding." For example, the man who says, too casually, "I think I'll take . . . [pause, as if he's making a hard choice] . . . the Ford tonight," is trying to give the impression that there is more than one car in the family, and maybe even a garage-full. The question for you to determine (assuming you care) is whether or not it's so.

Possibly more apropos is the woman you ask to dinner; when she says she has to "look at her calendar" the inference one might draw is that she is terribly popular. However, she may not be busy at all, and knows it. In such a case, although she hasn't deliberately lied, hasn't she toyed just a little with the truth? Then there's the salesman, who threatens "they're going fast"; often he neglects to tell you that, even so, he can *always* fill your order. Or take the brochures I mentioned: "nearby" anything, for example, could be half an hour away. A "short drive to town" over winding hilly roads (not mentioned) can easily take an hour, plus twenty bucks for the cab (never mentioned). And "all facilities are on the premises" is meaningless: *what* facilities are they talking about? So read between even the printed lines, analytically and cynically; take the words at their most literal meanings and don't assume anything.

In this matter of language and meaning, therefore, you have to watch out for all of these misleading implications and innuendoes. You will recall my earlier suggestions to pinpoint and make as specific as possible the information you have been given and to use language clearly and precisely. The basic essential is the ability to listen, and then analyze and interpret what has in fact been said. In this regard there's a funny little saying I picked up somewhere in my travels; it goes like this: "I know you believe you understand what you think I said, but I'm not sure you realize that what you heard is *not* what I meant."

There's a lot of truth in that: if what you think you heard is not what was meant, then any understanding you base upon your erroneous thinking is bound to be wrong. You must be sure that you clearly comprehend what has actually been said and meant, neither more nor less. Therefore the words you are using must have the same meaning for both you and the person you are communicating with, or you are lost. It's difficult enough to make good decisions as it is; we don't need inaccuracies of language and meaning to make it more so. So don't hesitate to ask, frequently if necessary: "*Exactly* what does that mean?" or "Are you saying this?" And then paraphrase it, just to be sure. Don't ever be afraid or embarrassed to ask. If anything, most people will respect you the more for having been precise and pinning them down to specifics. And if they don't like it, that's *their* problem; you've got your own world to take care of.

You must also be sure to base your decision on the real cost to you, rather than only the apparent one. Businessmen know, for example, that it's not the price they pay for the new equipment that is meaningful; rather, what is important is its real cost after they adjust that figure on the basis of all the tax advantages they may take. Or, on a lesser level: suppose you are that person who needs the new bath towels. If, say, the cheapest one you can dry yourself off with costs two dollars, and the one you would love to have costs five, then the *real* cost of the preferred one is three dollars, not five, since you would have spent at least the two in either event. And so the decision between the two towels is whether your aesthetic satisfaction is worth three dollars.

The formula is simple: the minimum cost for the cheaper alternative, whatever it may be, has to be deducted from the cost of the more expensive one in order to find its real cost. Obviously the real cost of the cheaper one is the price you are actually paying for it.

Take, for example, a gambling situation: backgammon. When the doubling cube is offered to you, you have two choices: either to quit, and pay whatever the bet then is, or to play on, but now for double the original bet.

Let's assume the original bet is one dollar. Now, if you quit you *must* pay the one, but if you want to play on, you automatically accept the increase of the bet to two dollars. So, if you play on and finally lose, the actual cost of this gamble is only one dollar, since you would have had to pay the first dollar anyway, even if you quit. At the time of decision, the risk to you for the right to continue is one dollar, not two. (If you're a backgammon player, you may be interested to know that if you do play on under these circumstances, the possible outcome for you at this moment is to win three dollars, not two, for your one at risk. And I'm not talking about gammons or triple games, either. Read my book on the game for a detailed explanation of this, if you're interested.) The person who goes to Vegas and sets a limit on the amount he is prepared to lose at the gaming tables is doing it the right way; he may get ten or twenty times as much action because he plays and replays his winnings as well (his "handle," the total betting is called), but his real cost is only the amount he came with.

You also must recognize the cost of the status quo, where the real cost is not the apparent price of the alternative, but the difference between that and what you must pay to continue the present state of affairs. Suppose, for example, you are thinking of moving to a larger apartment: the real cost of the additional space is the rent you would have to pay there, less the amount you are now paying. Or maybe you're thinking of sending your child to camp. What would it cost you to feed, clothe, and entertain him for the summer at home, as opposed to this figure for camp? The net difference between the two is the real cost, not the apparent price of the camp itself. And the real cost of dinner at a restaurant is not the tab itself; it's that less the amount you would spend on your food and its preparation at home.

You have to figure your costs in the same way as best you can where the prices are psychological; you must have some idea of the meaning of various actions to you. Suppose, for example, you are considering ending a relationship, and know that by doing so you will suffer great pain. *That's* not the real cost; the bottom line on this one is the *extra* amount of pain (if any) you may suffer because of the split, over and beyond the torture of remaining together. It may be hard to measure such a subjective thing, but you must be sure you have at least an idea of the real cost, not the apparent one. So do your arithmetic carefully. Cost appraisal is a very important part of good decision making, and you don't want to make any mistakes in this matter.

You've now done the first part of the evaluation process: your information has been checked for its honesty, accuracy, reliability, truthfulness, and completeness. Now that you know you can trust this information and that it is valid, you must determine if you can use it. Does it have value? Is it meaningful and worthwhile? Does it have significance?

Essentially, in terms of evidence, this analysis involves two elements: materiality and relevance. Or, if you want it in trial terminology, and the way you hear it on television, be careful that it isn't immaterial and irrelevant. To be relevant, information must have some reasonable relationship to the matter you are considering; if it tends to throw any light upon the subject it is relevant. Of course, as I suggested earlier, you should have determined the relevancy of all your information before you wasted even a second on collecting it.

But materiality is the real key in decision making. Does this information have any pertinent bearing on the problem? How much value does it have? How much influence should it exert on your ultimate decision? And, of course, how do you determine this?

Obviously, "value" is only a relative word. It is so completely subjective that standards for measurement are patently impossible. As I pointed out earlier, what is important to one person may have no significance to another. Furthermore, someone may be greatly concerned about a particular piece of information in one situation and yet in another the same person won't even consider it. "Value" means different things at different times, and only you can judge the level of importance any specific item has to you. Such a judgment is totally individual, very much like the matter of psychological cost I discussed earlier. Therefore, I think it would be presumptuous of me to even try to suggest how you should determine the value of this information for yourself. I will only offer some working principles to be aware of and which may be of help as guides.

Paramount among these in determining the value of your information is a recognition of the quality of its source. If your information is from an individual, how good are his qualifications? What is his background in this field? Is this an area in which he has special knowledge, training, or experience? How did he get his information? How capable do you think he is? Is what he has to say really worthwhile? The mere fact that a person may know more about a subject than you do is not sufficient reason for him to offer an opinion or for you to accept it. It is only if he has a particular knowledge of the subject, or experience or expertise in it, that you should listen to him. You must always be careful not to waste your time and attention on a person who has nothing of particular value to offer. Examine his credentials closely if his ideas are of substantial importance in your evaluation; that is the only way to know if the information has any real value.

Similarly, you should also watch out for instant prophets and their sermons from the mount. These are people who have made their fame and fortune in a particular field, and probably for good reason. Then they hype themselves into believing that this feat has also conveyed upon them special powers in other, totally unrelated areas. They are like the carnival magician: he presents us with an illusion that is completely without a basis in fact, and then depends on us to fill in the substance that is lacking because we would like to believe him. And we, poor lambs, often do.

What I'm talking about is our tendency to worship heroes and to ascribe to them virtues that are in fact nonexistent. For example, a man may perform spectacular acts of courage and skill in a boxing ring; this does not mean that he knows any more about the problems of the Middle East than do you or I. His insights are not keener, his knowledge is not broader, and his intelligence may not even be as great. Why, then, should we pay the slightest attention to any of his political pronouncements? And my particular gripe is against those purveyors of charm who suddenly have become experts on practically everything. (Or, at least, practically anything that's commercial.) The idea that a guy who has a great passing arm with a football knows more about what people should smell like than, say, my dog, is a piece of sheer lunacy. In this area he's just another joe in the street for my money. Certainly the girls he attracts to his bedroom are not there because of his after-shave, and any suggestible fool who believes this tripe and buys this glop probably deserves to have his money taken from him in this fashion. It is really bizarre.

The point is that although these celebrities may be deservedly renowned for their exploits in a particular field, this does not mean that you should accept the implication that they know any more than you do about any *other* field. In fact, because they are so dedicated—and so committed—to their careers, they probably know less simply because they have less time than you to think about anything else. They remind me of my debate coach's definition of a so-called expert, whose opinions were being used against us in one match. "An expert," he drawled, "is only a little spurt a long way from home."

So beware of experts, and testimonials, and people who sound off about things they really know little or nothing about. Such evidence is worth precisely that—little or nothing. Many people try to sound important; too often, however, their intelligence is not the equal of their ego needs. So question their contributions, and evaluate what they have to say on one basis only, and on it alone: is this an area in which this person qualifies as having special knowledge, or training, or ability? And if you judge it this way, you will know just what the ideas are worth. There *are* some experts around, and what they have to say can be very valuable. Be sure, however, that you're getting the genuine article and not the sideshow charlatan.

And be careful that you don't play expert. It's easy to ascribe to yourself abilities, or traits, or knowledge that you don't have; we all have some built-in cravings toward ego. On the other hand, you cannot be humble and demean your qualifications and talents. Either way you're in trouble. An inflated opinion of oneself will surely lead to disappointment and frustration, and probably also to a loss of friends. Conversely, a bad self-image is usually self-fulfilling; they say that pessimists are never disappointed.

The key is self-awareness: you must evaluate yourself carefully and know yourself honestly, and realistically, and well. And if you're not absolutely sure of the accuracy of your self-appraisal, use the same kind of cross-examination on yourself that you did on the others. Also examine your own history and experiences to see what might be similar or related—good or bad. You might want to re-read the chapters on self-respect to see if any of the problems are now pertinent. Or get a good friend—one who knows you well—to help. Just keep in mind that self-questioning of this sort can be as valuable to you in coming to good decisions as is the questioning of others.

In a way the matter of evaluating all comes down to something said to me by a friend over dinner. She is a reporter for a suburban paper, and since it is not published in my area, I was not familiar with her work. I asked her how satisfied she was with what she was doing, and she replied that she didn't think she was very good at it.

"Why not?" I asked.

"Because I'm not suspicious enough yet," she replied. "But I'm getting there."

And so can you. Just keep questioning. Everything.

13

Deliberation and Decision

On the desk in my office is a crystal ball, a real honest-to-god one, which I bought from a Hungarian gypsy many years ago. I don't pretend to know how to read it, but it serves a purpose. When clients say, in an attempt to minimize my time and consequently my bill, "Please don't make it one of your long contracts," I merely indicate the globe and ask them to tell me what will not happen so I can then leave out the paragraphs covering those possibilities. Sheepishly, they withdraw the request.

If only we could read that crystal ball: what a blessing! We could see all our future actions, and we would know their consequences. Life would be easier, and simpler, and presumably even more fun.

But, although you can buy crystal balls, you cannot buy the

power to read them. So you are forced to fend for yourself. You must make your own decisions, only without the benefit of knowing what should be concentrated on, and what can safely be left out of consideration. Therefore this is a time for careful deliberation and thorough analysis; it is the moment of truth. And that's the point you have reached: you must now deliberate, and then decide.

Deliberation is the act of weighing and balancing the reasons for and against each option in order to select the one best suited to your needs. It is the process of using your intelligence to interpret the information you have collected and assimilated, and then, based on this evaluation, carefully and thoroughly calculating the consequences of your possible courses of action so that you can choose the particular one that is most likely to be best for you. And, unless your decision is purely a right-brain one, a certain amount of deliberation always takes place before you make your choice.

And it is smart to deliberate: it is a lot easier, and a lot cheaper in terms of the emotional price you have to pay, if you intelligently think your decision through before acting on it than if you try to correct a mistake once you have made it. As Shaw said, you should "choose the lines of greatest advantage instead of yielding to the path of least resistance." Let's talk about how to do this.

Essentially, you look for overall meanings by relying on your common sense and your reason; here is where you put your logic to use. Fortunately, you are now well prepared. You have done an enormous amount of work and collected a complete dossier of pertinent and evaluated information to help you in your decision. Now you have to take this information of varying quality and an unequal degree of relevance and intelligently meld it into a comprehensible and valid whole. You must maintain a proper perspective by selecting and focusing in on the pertinent material, while excluding that which is of no relevance. The process is one of discrimination (which is not a dirty word when used properly, such as here). This critical faculty can prevent you from getting bogged down in and inundated with too much to think about. T. S. Eliot said, "Where's the knowledge we lost with information?"; the thought is, unfortunately, too true.

Be careful, however, that you don't lose sight of the forest by concentrating on the trees. Keep your sense of proportion in a proper balance. Examine all dimensions of each factor we are about to discuss, and objectively and realistically evaluate them. Then ask yourself: What does this mean? How does it all relate? As Gide said, "There is always a struggle between what is reasonable and what is not." So you speculate, and you evaluate, and you draw the meaningful inferences. And your answer must be based on the objectively arrived at judgment: *this is probably the case*. In the absence of absolutes, this is obviously the best that you can do. But if you do it well, you can be sure that, without a reasonable doubt, this *is* the situation, and you can therefore depend on it.

Remember, too, that your right brain must also be satisfied; that the best decisions you can make are those which you both arrive at after significant logical thought and which also *feel* comfortable. And if you don't have the right feelings, or if the "vibrations" are bad, beware! Re-examine all your information very carefully, for you are getting a clear right-brain warning that you have probably fallen into a trap somewhere along the line. As I have continually pointed out, the right brain must be used to supplement, corroborate, and confirm the activity of the left. The two sides must be in harmony as you do this deliberation, or you can be sure that you are doing it badly, and will come up with the wrong decisions.

Good decisions are nothing more or less than value judgments based on your own subjective point of view and your own objective determination of the relative worth of the information you have. It is left-brain and right-brain awareness and intelligence, both intellectually and emotionally acceptable. You must satisfy your logic, and you must also satisfy your instinct. First, your decision must meet the crucial test of logic: does it make sense? Or, even better, the ultimate trial: will it make sense tomorrow? And it must also meet the right-brain test: does it *feel* right? And will it, too, feel right tomorrow? And your choice, based upon these considerations, is now a highly informed prediction and substantially more than a hope that a desired result will occur.

To "choose" means to select one course of action in preference to all other possibilities which, obviously, must be foregone. This process of selection and exclusion is what sets up the conflict;

being human we don't want to give up anything, particularly when we are not quite sure what it is that we may be losing. But we must, by the process of choice, and when the stakes are high the result for many people is anger or frustration or aggression. These are often coupled with withdrawal and poor performance. Generally, this is then even further compounded by all the anxieties that go into making a change—the fears, the insecurities, the guilt; all the baggage of our childhood. To top it all off, your basic, underlying emotion is a desire to achieve the best for yourself. So you're torn apart; the thought of making a decision can easily become more terrifying than the decision itself. And, unfortunately, the resulting tension is a self-perpetuating spiral; the tenser you are, the more tense you will get. And the apprehension is also self-fulfilling: when you're fearful of making a mistake, you're virtually certain to do so.

So the best thing to do in order to make better decisions is to relax. And it's easy: now all the steps and efforts that you have gone through to get to this point, all the wealth of information and material you have gathered, will stand you in good stead. They are invaluable tools to help put you at ease. You *know* that your decisions are going to be better both because you are no longer such willing prey to the conflicting emotions you suffered before, and because you are so much better prepared to deal with your problems. And this feeling of self-confidence will be partially responsible for the deed. When you believe you can make better decisions, it will be easier to do so.

But don't get any delusions of grandeur. You have not yet become a seer; you *still* can't read that crystal ball. You will still make mistakes; unfortunately, to err will always be a human way of life. Again, however, this awareness of human fallibility will help you relax; you're not expected to be perfect. But I did promise you that you will make fewer bad decisions, and that's your security. Just don't panic when (not if) you do make a wrong choice; assuredly you will still make mistakes, but you will progressively make less and less of them. Remember that you cannot control the outcome of your decisions. There are too many external factors that can influence or change the results of any decision, no matter how well-made, and so even with your most competent appraisal of the future, you will sometimes find the outcome wanting. Chance is ever-present. Sometimes it helps, and sometimes it hurts.

Therefore you must always be aware of the possibility that your decision may be a flop, and you must be emotionally prepared for it. Don't take such a wrong outcome personally, thereby allowing it to add to or exacerbate any feelings of insecurity you have. Instead, use your awareness of possible failure in your decision making. The Boy Scout motto is "Be Prepared." I presume that this is for Murphy's Law, which says, "If something can go wrong, it will." Actually, I do not believe Mr. Murphy; his is one of those broad aphorisms that sound cleverer than they really are. But Murphy's Law has value in that it serves as a cynical reminder of a potential underlying all our decisions, and it is precisely because of this element of chance that you have to be prepared for this possibility of failure. How to best deal with this is something I will get to shortly. And, with this security, you will be better able to relax and, consequently, make better decisions.

Time is another important element contributing to your mental relaxation. Earlier, in talking about priorities, I cautioned about taking too much of this precious item for any matter. Now I will offer the converse of this admonition: when the problem is of sufficient significance, be sure to take enough time. Gestation is a necessary ingredient in all creative activity, and what can be more vital than a decision that may affect the whole course of your life? Remember, you're making a choice, not constructing a clock. So take as much time as you need to think, and to consider, and to deliberate. Assume the freedom to listen to yourself; in fact, *insist* on it. Don't allow others to pressure you. It's *your* moment of truth, not anyone else's. If they have to wait while you take care of yourself, that's their problem and not your concern. And, by knowing that you have given yourself the temporal space in which to do your thinking, you will be more relaxed in making your decisions.

You will also find it helpful if you can do this deliberation at what may be your optimum time for such functioning. Studies in the field of biorhythm suggest that at certain times of the day we function better, both mentally and physically, than we do at other periods; there are morning people, and afternoon people, and there are others for whom the day is just one long siesta. The vital functions of the body and the brain seem to have these cyclical characteristics and, although they vary from person to person, they remain fairly consistent for each individual. Therefore you should try to be aware of your own behavior pattern and its better moments, and use them to your advantage.

You can encourage the deliberation process. You should do your thinking when you are physically in the best of circumstances; this in itself is always a big help. You should be in a quiet and calm mood if possible. Try to avoid distractions, strong emotional feelings (that are not related to the matter being decided), and other impediments to your concentration. Preferably you should also be rested and physically well. The ancient Greek ideal was "a sound mind in a sound body," and our modern-day research merely confirms that the mind is a better functioning mechanism when the body is well. A lack of sleep or a deficiency in diet (and especially protein) can be conducive to poor functioning; many bad decisions are made because of fatigue and even brain malnutrition. On the other hand, your mental processes will be enhanced when your physical ones are in good condition; the adrenalin will flow better, the energy level to deal with your problems will be higher, and your mind will function more quickly and efficiently. This, by the way, is a desirable level of excitement and should not be confused with tension. So, for the best decisions, be rested. Be properly fed. And be relaxed.

Essentially you want to decide on that course of action which is most likely to give you the outcome you want. However, almost invariably such a choice involves a certain cost, even if this is nothing more than the alternatives you have to forego. Further, it involves a certain risk—what can happen to you, what is the price you will have to pay, if the outcome is not successful? Consequently you must consider and evaluate these various factors, so that you can come up with the best decision under all the possible circumstances.

Some of the management books I mentioned earlier are replete with formulas for this. Everything gets assigned a letter or a number, and maybe even an exponent; then it gets put through a series of complicated algebraic computations that have been dreamed up by the writer. Although I don't pretend to be a mathematical genius, as some of these experts do, I did get through calculus in college and I have some small confidence with numbers. And so I tried several of these, hoping they might be of value. Unfortunately, however, I must reluctantly report that in my opinion these formulas are at best totally impractical and at worst sheer hypocrisy. The only purpose I can see for any of these books is to possibly impress some poor young thing who sees one on your bookshelf, and naively may think you've read it. However, panic not; I will tell you how I put it all together, and how you can too.

The first thing you must ask yourself at this point, without regard for any of the other aspects of the question, is which of the various possibilities that are available to you will make you most happy, assuming that your choice will be successful?

What do you most want for you?

I want to be very explicit here: I am specifically saying that at this moment you should deliberately ignore the cost and risk factors that are present. You first must know this one particular, isolating it from all other considerations: if the only thing that matters is what you want *most*, which of these options will give it to you?

Earlier I spoke of the two basic categories of decision making, one being the question of "Yes or no" and the other the issue of "Which one?" In general, both can be decided on the basis of the most preferable option because, as I pointed out, the two methods are essentially the same. In either situation you must choose one of the available alternatives. The fact that in the yes-or-no situation one of the options is actually allowing the status quo to continue is of no material consequence at present. You still have to decide which alternative you prefer. And, based upon all you now know: your goals, your options, and the pertinent information you have gathered about each and put into its proper perspective, you can usually say which of these you most desire. If you have clearly delineated your goals, and you are sure that your short-range quantitative goals are at least in harmony with your long-range qualitative ones, you should easily be able to determine the one course of action that is most in conformity with them.

It is possible, of course, that this is purely a right-brain feeling as to which you prefer. That's fine, since all matters of preference must ultimately satisfy this side of your intelligence or fail. And it is also possible that you have known this all along; the additional knowledge you have gained has merely corroborated this choice. But whether you have merely confirmed the original inclination, or you have come to another preferred course of action because of what you have since discovered, you are now in the enviable position of really knowing what it is that you most want. Clearly, as a result of all your investigation and information and evaluation, you can truly say with confidence and conviction, based on solid knowledge, that this choice, rather than any other, is the one that will most likely give you happiness. And that, of course, is always the ultimate goal.

And so, with this preferred course of action firmly in mind, you are now ready for my Famous Fast Formula (for fame and fortune). It's breathtaking in its simplicity, it's startling in its obviousness, and it's amazing in its success. But don't underestimate it. In spite of its seeming naiveté, the formula is extremely profound. It is:

> Provided that you don't veto it, this preferred course of action is your choice!

Think about it: why shouldn't it be your decision if that's what will give you the most happiness? Following your preferred course of action really makes sense.

Of course, there is that veto provision, which implies certain questions about this choice. That, unfortunately, is the rub. (It is also your Security Council.) What does it mean, you rightly ask? Why should the grand desire be vetoed?

Well, all kidding aside, this is the point at which the other factors come into account—the cost, the probability of success, and the risk. You must consider them now, for any one of these matters may be sufficient to act as a veto of your primary choice. And the beauty of the system is the ease with which you can now consider your decision, and the assuredness with which you can choose. If you have properly done the necessary preparation for this moment of truth, it will be very hard to make a mistake because the procedure itself is very simple.

The choice you make is the choice you want, provided that its cost is not too high, nor its risk too great, nor its chances of success too small.

And you have all this pertinent and relevant information, carefully collected and evaluated; now all you have to do is use it intelligently. Here you must be very realistic, and logical, and practical; you must make as objective an appraisal of each of these factors as you possibly can.

The order in which you consider these elements is of no practical concern, since each is equally important in your final decision. I generally think about the cost factor first, however. You will recall that this is the price you have to pay if you take this course of action, as well as its continuing demands as a result of this decision. What this cost may be—whether in terms of money, time, energy, or emotional commitment—is something you have already carefully thought out; now you merely have to apply this information.

The way to do it is easy: you simply have to ask yourself whether or not this choice, still assuming it will turn out successfully, is worth this price. Are you capable of paying it, and are you prepared to do so? And are you willing to accept the future responsibility for it? There is no room for equivocation: the answer is either yes or no. As you can see, the question is so clear and clean that you cannot say "maybe" or "it depends"; any such vagueness is merely procrastination or, worse, avoidance. You really can't get down to a more basic issue: are you willing to pay this price for this choice (which *is* your primary desire), if you have the assurance and understanding that it will be successful?

You may not be absolutely sure of your feelings about this, and in such an event I suggest that you try to make a list of the costs. Here again, as before, the simple matter of putting pencil to paper will help your left brain work better, and you will get more clarity in your thinking. Put down the costs, preferably dividing them into two areas: present and future. And, if it is helpful, you might even go one step further: separate the definite, absolute costs from those that are more speculative but are potentially present and therefore must also be considered. With this list, you then should be able to clearly and accurately answer the question of whether or not you're willing to pay the probable price.

Of course, the price must be a healthy one. We all know people who tend to the self-destructive; they seem to always want what they just as often should not have. Their men continually dump on them; their women are demanding princesses; their friends are selfish and inconsiderate. However, I must assume that you are not party to such masochism and that you can now recognize what is a dangerous course of conduct and avoid it. Therefore, on the premise that you are intelligently choosing that which you should do, and which will best achieve your ultimate happiness, the question: supposing for the moment that the option you desire will be successful, is it worth the price you have to pay?

You can see where this leads. If your answer is yes, that the cost *is* worth it, you can now forget this factor and go on to the rest of your deliberation. The preferred option has met this test. If, however, the answer is no, the cost is *not* worth it, you have in effect vetoed the primary choice. And it is only you—and you alone, based on your own evaluations—who must decide whether or not you are willing to pay this price in order to go ahead with your choice.

If you do veto this option because of its cost, or you later do so because of one of the other factors yet to be considered, you then go through the same process for your second most appealing option. What is *its* cost, and is it worth the price? Obviously, if that too doesn't pass muster, then you go to the third. And so on. The procedure is extremely simple; the only problem may be that all your options flunk this test. But if this should happen, you can be sure that you have either defined your problem incorrectly or you have not recognized all your alternatives. In such event, you had better examine your earlier thinking much more carefully. You might even re-read the pertinent sections of this book; it is just possible you overlooked something.

Let's stay with the first possibility. Let's accept that you believe this option is worth the price you must pay to choose it; this conclusion was based on the stipulated assumption that you expect this alternative to succeed. Now, let's test *that* assumption: what *are* its chances of success? Do you think it is more likely to be favorable in its outcome, or unfavorable? How likely is it to be the right decision? And, once again, you possess an abundance of pertinent information about this aspect of the problem and this option. All the material can now be weighed so that you can effectively and sensibly predict with a reasonable probability of success what this alternative offers. It is true that this is often a subjective factor, yet you do know enough about your alternative to have what can be called an informed opinion as to this probability. Certainly your prediction represents much more than just a guess. Even if you call what you are relying on instinct or intuition, that's still a part of your intelligence at work.

So deliberate about this option, considering the relevant facts you know about it, and come up with an answer to the basic question: does it have better than an even chance of being successful? That, for me, is the criterion: if this alternative has more than a 50–50 chance of working out the way I want it to, it is good enough. Even the slightest edge is sufficient; just as long as there is better than an even chance of success, that's my choice.

You may wish to change the numbers from 50–50, and look for somewhat better than this dividing line; however, although it is your formula to do with as you wish, I think a different ratio is unrealistic. A higher degree of achievement may be desired and even looked for, but in general if you have better than an even chance of success for your most desired option, you're in fine shape. If you project this ratio, it means that in your next hundred decisions, say, you will have your first choice in more than half of them (at least as far as this factor is concerned). And I think that such a percentage is certainly more than acceptable. These are gambler's odds; any professional will settle right now, and for forever, on this split. I refer you again to the casinos at Vegas and elsewhere around the world, where fortunes have been made for their owners on as small an advantage as 51 to 49. This dividing line also has the benefit of simplicity: it is much easier to predict than, say, a 60–40 or a 70–30 split. So I strongly urge this better-than-even ratio as your basic test; it really works.

But whatever your numbers, the principle is clear and simple: if your option passes this test, and you are satisfied that it has a reasonably good chance of success, then it's on to the next question. If it doesn't pass and gets vetoed, then back to "Go," to similarly test option number two.

The last factor you must consider is the risk—what may happen to you if this option does *not* work out. What are the dangers? What can you lose? And then, of course, you must be willing to take this risk. Nor is there anyone who can tell you how much of a risk to assume, or how important it can be; this is a highly subjective matter, and only you can make the evaluation for yourself.

What I do here is ask myself: what is the *worst* that can happen? And, if it should be a disaster, can I handle it? For example, the woman who was asked to be patient in her career knew that her impatience in pressing the matter would, at worst, cost her that job. It was conceivable that her employers would fire her on the theory that she had lost the necessary interest in her work. If, however, she did not get the promotion she wanted, she probably would have quit anyway, thus putting herself in exactly the same position of being out of an unrewarding situation. Consequently, in effect there was no risk, and so she was perfectly calm in forcing the issue. Similarly, another person I know who was able to support herself realized that the worst that could happen to her if she chose divorce was loneliness and boredom; that risk, she felt, was still preferable to what she was living with.

Therefore you must analyze this risk factor and fully understand and appreciate the worst that can possibly occur. You then are faced with the question of whether you can live with that eventuality, or if you find it instead too frightening or painful a prospect. If you feel you can accept the risk, then your preferred option has passed its last test. If, however, you are not willing to take the chance, then you have probably vetoed this choice and you must now consider the next preference instead.

There is, however, a way of reducing the risk of failure, as I said earlier. In most aspects of life you can obtain insurance; in fact, you can buy it to protect against certain contingencies even at the blackjack table. And insurance is what I have in mind here. You can achieve peace of mind about your risks by knowing very clearly what your fall-back position will be should your decision be unsuccessful. In effect, you must be prepared at all times for the possibility of failure; you must know, should your choice not work out, what you can then do. It is surprising how often this safety valve is overlooked, and at what a cost! A well-formulated fall-back position is one of the best pieces of preparation you can have, so you would be well advised to always keep it in mind. It may be a return to the present status quo, or it may be your next most preferable option. And even if this backstop is not too desirable, it will always serve to mitigate the danger of failure.

So be prepared: always know how you can minimize your risk. Having such security may make certain actions less dangerous and therefore more palatable, thereby allowing you to choose an option that is higher in preference. And, in turn, more of your decisions will consequently turn out right; this kind of confidence is both self-perpetuating and self-fulfilling. Nothing is as comforting as knowing that you're well-prepared.

That's the easy way to do it. You choose the highest-ranking option—the one that is the most desirable to you—that meets the following criteria: (1) its price is one you are willing to pay; (2) it has a reasonable probability of success; and (3) the risk of its possible failure is one you can at least live with. Very simple, and practically foolproof. And, of course, you always have your fall-back position.

There is one other possibility I'd like to discuss: the one in which your goal is clear, but you're just not sure which of two options—or even several—will best achieve this particular goal. When you are in this situation, I suggest that you should first examine this determination on the basis of *both* your qualitative and quantitative goals. It seems highly unlikely that none of your options will be a more preferable one when the two areas of goals are considered. Although two or more of these alternatives may at times seem equally likely to achieve your short-range desires, generally one or the other will be the preferred one when it is measured against your long-range qualitative goals. Or vice-versa. And so this should determine your choice.

However, you still may not be clear on an option that is most desirable. In such a situation, how do you choose? Well, here the procedure varies, but only a bit. What you now must do is rank in order of importance the three criteria you are using: the cost, the probability of success, and the risk. You must carefully think about these factors and determine which of these three is of most consequence and concern to you in this situation. Then, you should test the competing options to see which is the preferable alternative when you are considering them in terms of this most important standard. If your alternatives still come up fairly evenly matched, do the same with the next most important factor, and then even the third. This ranking *should* do it.

But let's assume the worst—after all this painstaking analysis, you *still* can't decide. You have carefully taken all these steps and everything has properly passed the test. One way or another, you come out at the end with more than one possibility, and these are so equally balanced in their basic values that you find it impossible to make a choice. Although I believe that you probably have overlooked or shortchanged one of the steps, so that the matter has not been as carefully analyzed and considered as it should be, I will help you out of this dilemma. All you have to do is flip a coin.

That's what I said.

Just throw a coin high in the air.

Then, while it's up there, spinning brightly, and in the split second before the coin lands, pick an alternative.

That's the one. Forget everything else and *simply let your right brain decide*. That's your choice. And you really can't make a horrendous mistake, you know, because the entire situation has now been so carefully thought out, and the options you're flipping between *are* so evenly matched, that whichever one you choose will certainly be at least as good as any other. Probably it will even be better, for it will have the great advantage of being your intuitive choice—which at this stage of the game is surely the best guarantee of its preferability.

In a certain sense, this is exactly what happens when you are faced with questions that have strong emotional overtones. In such situations there is no information or evaluation or deliberation that is possible, or acceptable, or desired. Your first reaction is often your final decision: it is a right-brain absolute. You know your feelings; these are generally very strong, and they are all that matter. The choice is easy. Things like the landing rights for the Concorde, or building nuclear power plants, fall into this area. The question is really a sociological one: What risks should be accepted in exchange for the benefits? With how much uncertainty does one care to live? Obviously this is a very subjective—and emotional—matter. It's intuitive, and you decide accordingly—even if you have very little to say, or little you can do, about the problem. I mention this only so that you are aware of this kind of right-brain decision, and you therefore don't spend too much time in deliberating about it. You're going one way or the other, and that's it. Done.

The same kind of subjective decision making can take place even if the matter is not emotionally oriented. For example, an editor I know makes up her mind about the commercial viability of a manuscript after quickly reading through only a few pages. Her decision is based upon her years and years of experience. The accumulated wisdom of this background is all there in her right brain ready to be combined with the other right-brain attribute called taste to make this virtually instant judgment. My friend has learned how to short-circuit many of the steps that a less experienced editor would have to go through more painstakingly; in effect she has paid her dues and is now profiting from her education. And she, dear woman, misnames it: she tells her editorial board that "I know in my gut" that this will, or will not, make it. But the important thing is that she has an exceptional average; when she speaks of her intuitive feelings, everyone listens. Similarly, you can do the same thing at certain times; you have enough accumulated wisdom of your own so that you instinctively know just what you should do in these various areas.

The same kind of decision making can also help when you're taking a test and you don't have sufficient time to think out the answers to all the questions—or you're not sure what the answers are, even after thinking. If the questions are the true-false kind, or multiple choice, do the same kind of trick as the one I suggested before with the coin: simply run through the list very quickly, and put down the answer that comes first to your mind. This is right-brain awareness, and psychological tests have proven that you will be correct considerably more often than not if you follow this procedure. As I have continually been emphasizing, the right brain is a phenomenal tool, and you must learn how to use it—and then allow yourself to do so.

Of course, the human factor is always present. There are ways to muck up a decision and create some havoc. I'd like to talk about a few so that you are better prepared to deal with them. Essentially, all these go back to the matter of self-respect I discussed earlier —the programming by our authority figures; our insecurities and fears of failure (or success); our desire to be loved; the whole mess. These are, for the most part, unhealthy emotional needs, and decisions that are mainly the result of these cravings are virtually certain to be bad. You know as many examples as I of people who, merely out of loneliness, will date anyone who calls, and then hate themselves afterward for having done so. The fantasy, of course, is that one of these losers will be *it*, with happiness ever after as the destined end. Remaining in a bad relationship—or any situation—because of a baseless hope that "maybe it will get better" is another example of a poor decision.

It is exactly this kind of wishful thinking that can intrude on the decision making process and ruin it, even at this stage. In spite of all the careful work that you have done up to now, you have to constantly separate fiction from fact, and you have to be aware that the hope that springs eternal in the human breast is, unfortunately, usually only that and nothing more. Hope is fine and dandy, and we all need it and live with it; however, it is not the proper substance of wise decisions.

Unrealistic expectations color situations and change their meaning; such fanciful thinking often gives birth to repeated disappointments. Expectations make us see things that aren't there or blind us to facts that are. We want it to be, and so we fantasize it *will* be. Optical illusions and carnival magicians effectively use this principle of expectation, and it is perfectly appropriate for such fun and games; when we carry this rationalization over into real life, however, the results are not so amusing. We sometimes will invent an explanation because we are unconsciously trying to justify a particular point of view. We may set up false obstacles simply to rationalize that which we want to believe. Or we may twist the interpretation of the facts or even ignore a piece of information that may tend to discredit that which we wish to believe. It is difficult—although very human—to accept information that runs counter to our preconceptions and our desires, and it is extremely easy to allow rationalizations to control our decisions.

People do this all the time; we are all clever at convincing ourselves. We follow custom, and we repeat past mistakes, all through this rationalization. Businessmen will manufacture enthusiasm and convince themselves that a deal is better than it really is. Partnerships continue because of a false hope; stocks are bought this way; lonely people enter—and remain in—unhappy relationships. And our society tends to accept this insufficiency: you've often heard the line "we don't always do what we'd like to do." That's nonsense, and should be relegated to the garbage pail; provided only that you don't encroach on another's rights you always should—and must—do only what you want to do.

In your deliberations, therefore, you must always be careful that you recognize and deal in reality; don't be guilty of self-hype. Keep in mind what Bertrand Russell once said: "It is undesirable to believe a proposition when there is no ground for supposing it true." So the admonition is clear: don't rationalize. Face up to, accept, and deal in reality.

Similarly, you must be careful not to rationalize inertia. I know a woman who moved from New York to Atlanta, hoping that the change of scene would help her get her head together. Of course, her problems went with her and were still ever-present; she obviously was not dealing with her real, underlying troubles. Decisions such as hers are based on the emotional desire to escape a situation, yet without really understanding it. And this avoidance then deteriorates into a matter of grabbing at the first apparent alternative, without recognizing that this is not a genuine option to satisfy the real need, but is only an outlet for wishful thinking. I did the same when I started law school, remember? Obviously, you must face up to the problem, not run from it. The decision you make must be responsive to the need.

You must also be careful that you are not pressured or manipulated into making a decision that you don't want for yourself.

Reacting to someone else's temper tantrum may do this to you. Allowing guilt of one kind or another to influence your decision is also a danger. So is doing something merely because it is expected of you. I know a man who took a job he didn't really want because of insidious influences from his dominating parents. I have known others who went into unwanted relationships for the same reasons. Or the reverse can happen: often people who resent being dictated to (whatever shape it takes) will attempt to resist this authority by doing the exact opposite of what they think is expected, all the while being just as manipulated by their own defiance as the person who does what is demanded of him. All these people then rationalize their behavior, trying to convince us—and themselves—that they did the wisest thing.

These attitudes, and the actions based upon them, are the emotional baggage of our childhood and must be kept from intruding into the decision-making process. You must have confidence in yourself, and in your decisions, so that you can avoid the biggest danger of all: the lack of commitment. You must be bold enough to have the courage of your convictions. Having decided on your best course of action, you must now act on it.

Which is the next step.

14

Acting on Your Decision

At a dinner party, a lawyer I know was talking to another guest, who raised a common problem. This man, a doctor, was complaining about the people who approached him at similar dinners and, on the pretext of making small talk, proceed to "mention" a symptom or two they were currently experiencing. This of course, was merely an introduction to the question of what they should do about it. The lawyer sympathized, and added that the same continually happened to him.

"What do you do about it?" asked the doctor, to whom this practice had obviously become quite troublesome.

"Send them a bill," the lawyer said. "A small one, but enough so that they'll get the message and not bother you again when you're out socially."

189

The doctor asked if this didn't really annoy some individuals, to which the lawyer replied that those who might be offended were not people you'd want to know anyway, and in any event the real problem was to rid oneself of such scavenging. Therefore, whatever way this might be done effectively should be used, and let the chips fall where they may. Upon reflection, the doctor agreed enthusiastically and announced that, beginning with this very dinner party, he would do the same; he thanked my lawyer friend effusively for this great help.

The next day the attorney sent him a bill for professional services rendered.

But the tag of the story—and the reason it's appropriate to begin this chapter—is that our lawyer had not done this before; he had never gotten up the nerve to act on his untested decision as to how to end these nuisance situations. However, the doctor's reaction to his suggestion convinced him that the idea was at least worth trying; the subsequent prompt payment of this bill then encouraged him to continue the practice, invariably with great success.

That's the point: a decision is of no value at all until, and unless, it is acted upon. But then, if it has been as carefully thought out as it should be, it can have great value. However, for some of us, to take action is the hardest step of all. We get up to this point and we seem to freeze. We go to the refrigerator, we call a friend, we feel sorry for ourselves; we vacillate and procrastinate and do anything and everything except face up to the act itself. The doing of the deed may be frightening, for the action to effect a decision always requires a commitment: whether of energy, money, time, or love; and the unknown can be ominous. Or the action may be painful if something you now have has to be given up, such as a lover, or parents, or a job; a move of this sort can be almost like the death of part of your life. So because of all the insecurities, or the fears, or the simple desire to avoid responsibility, it is not easy to act on everything you decide to do, and therefore you must have both the courage of your convictions and the motivation to carry them out. To achieve these requires two conditions: you must be willing to take responsibility for yourself, and you must want to accomplish your goal.

Accepting responsibility for yourself can be very difficult. I know many people who have decided to do something for themselves: lose weight, get a better job, end the bad affair, whatever. They then keep refusing to get the action underway, seemingly unwilling to realize that in effect they are instead merely allowing the status quo to continue. Or the procrastination gets explained away: A woman I know swears she wants to stop smoking, for example, but claims that if she does she will eat like a horse and become fat. And for her, she says, smoking is the lesser evil. But because of the guilt this rationalization has caused, she is over-eating as well, thereby hurting herself in both ways.

It is hard to want for yourself, and do for yourself; we've already talked about the reasons for this at great length in terms of the question of self-respect. But that's what you must do; you must say "I want" and "I will," and you must do that which you know should be done, and that which you have carefully and thought-fully decided to do. You must think of the commitment not as an ending but, rather, a beginning—and a healthy one at that. In effect, you must take charge of your destiny and take care of yourself. You must be self-dependent and self-reliant and, above all, self-respectful. No one else will do it for you; you must do it for yourself. In essence, the commitment is to you.

The heart of any action is communication; it is the indispens-able ingredient. To communicate means to make known; to impart or convey knowledge or information. And that's exactly what you do: you must make known your decision. You have to transmit this information to whomever may be involved in it; *that* is the necessary action. It need not be spoken, nor are words of any kind necessary; the communication may be merely by some physical indication, or it may be by doing the act itself. Even if the decision is internal, and the outcome affects only you, you must make the commitment by communicating it to yourself.

But it is absolutely essential that you always clearly understand what it is you have decided, and so must the person or people with whom you are dealing. This communication can be on the simplest of levels, such as the transaction involved in buying a towel; it can be the lawyer sending the doctor a bill; or it can deal with the most complex of human relationships. But in some way the commitment must be communicated, even if it goes no further than your own awareness. This is the essence of any action.

Think about it for a moment: without the communication of the commitment, the action can not be taken. "I quit," whether said, thought, or started; "I will buy that"; "I will stop smoking"; "I want you to pay me for my time"; "I will move in with you." Whether to yourself, or to others, the communication is necessary. There isn't a decision possible in which the action is not communicated in some fashion, and therefore what you must do is to somehow make the statement, so that you can then perform the act.

Further, when dealing with others, the clearer and more direct you are in your communication of your commitment, the less chance there is of your decision being misunderstood. And, therefore, it has that much better a chance of being successful. Communication is an art, possibly the most difficult one ever, and it depends not only on you but also on the listener. The transmission of ideas can fail in many ways, and although I have pointed out several of the problems in terms of your reception of ideas, so that you already have some awareness of these dangers, you will find that communication is always such a very difficult thing that you can never let down your guard. You must always be extra cautious that you are clearly understood. Attorneys—even though trained in semantics and the logical use of words—continually find themselves in court, fighting about their intended meanings. And if lawyers have so much trouble, you've got to expect it too.

Therefore, don't assume anything. Never delude yourself into believing that other people know what you are thinking. Even if you say it clearly, they often are not sure of your intent, and for you to hope that they understand unspoken thoughts is fantasy bordering on madness. Learn to communicate your decisions clearly, succinctly, directly. Say *exactly* what it is that you want, or will do, so that there is as little chance of misunderstanding as possible.

For example, when I was looking for a house in the country I told a real estate agent what I wanted. She assured me that my trip to her town would be worth my while for she had "exactly" what I wanted. But after I saw three houses that had virtually no resemblance to my dream I realized that communication between us had not happened. And so I interrupted her tour to explain that I was not interested in what she had to sell, but only in what I had decided to buy. If she had such a property, she would also have a sale; if not, we were both wasting our time. And I offered to tell her again exactly what I wanted if she cared to listen, which she did. Then, after assuring me once more that she had "exactly" the right thing, she proceeded to take me directly to the house I immediately bought. Communication did—and does—work.

It's probably more difficult in relationships, where two people have to be satisfied. What you must do in such matters—when you begin to date, or to love, or to live with—is to set the ground rules of the game. You must communicate—each to the other—as precisely as possible what the expectations, and the needs, and the demands are. Having these clearly spelled out in advance will help ensure that the decision to relate as well as the relationship itself will have a better chance of making it. There is now a big business in cohabitation contracts, for exactly this purpose. Putting down on paper (for the sake of both clarity and memory) precisely what the couple understand their mutual responsibilities to be is of enormous value in making the affair a happier one. You might want to do this for yourself.

Unquestionably, ground rules—and the communication of them—are invaluable in making many decisions work. And not only are they the basis of your self-respect, they are also a blessing to the people involved with you. There is less chance of misunderstanding; there is less chance of hurt. By simply saying to someone—child, friend, co-worker, lover, anyone—that this is what you have decided, and therefore this is acceptable to you and that is not, is to give them a clear picture of where you stand and what you demand. For remember, the ground rules that you set forth must be your own, based on your needs, and all you can ask from the others involved with you is that they either accept them, or not. In effect you are saying that this is your game, and these are your rules; if they want to play with you, they must abide by these rules. And if they don't like the rules, they can get out of the game.

I do not mean to imply that these needs and demands are always unilateral. Where two people are involved—as in a relationship—the ground rules must be jointly set, jointly understood, and jointly agreed to, if the game is to work at all. But I emphasize that you must be satisfied with them for yourself; that is your responsibility, both to yourself and to the other. In a sense you are saying that your decision is, simply: "I will go this far, and no farther; do with this information what you will."

Or possibly you may be in a situation where certain rules of behavior are imposed on you; for example, a hostess at a restaurant I frequent was fired for such a breach when she went out with one of the customers. However, by accepting a job, you in effect are accepting management's ground rules and making them your own. The important factor is to know these as well as you can *before* making the decision to accept the position so that you are not surprised or disappointed later. Again, communication is the key.

Or you may even ask for the rules to be imposed upon you in order to carry out your decision: that's precisely the advantage of joining Weight-Watchers, or Smoke-Enders, or outfits like these. Once you make the initial determination to lose weight or stop smoking, you communicate the decision by paying the fee. Thereafter you just follow what the authority figures tell you to do. Nor am I putting this down; often a crutch is necessary to effectuate a hard decision, and I am pragmatist enough to welcome this help from whatever the source. Of course it would be preferable if you could save the several hundreds of dollars and do this yourself without external pressure; however, if you find it easier to accomplish your goal by joining the group, then by all means do so. And the only piece of advice I will add is that you clearly understand and stringently follow their ground rules; these are all people who know what they're doing.

The communication of your decision can work for you in a different way; I call it witness-gathering. This is an old-time revival meeting means of ensuring that you will carry out your commitment by making it to others. It becomes a matter of pride: having said to these people that you are going to do a particular act, you will lose a lot of face if you don't perform as promised. And so, in a sense, you are forced into carrying out your decision. You must be careful here that you don't make this commitment only to close friends; they are sometimes too inclined to allow you to conveniently forget your decision if you find it to be troublesome. Make the commitment to people who know you and whom you respect and even fear just a bit; losing their regard may be too big a price to pay if you disappoint them.

One other warning: be careful that you don't communicate the commitment to downbeat people. There are many of these around, and they may unwittingly take the heart out of your decision by suggesting that you really don't think you're capable of *that*, do you? Or they'll keep nagging at you: haven't you accomplished it yet? Washington said, "It is better to be alone than in bad company," and this is appropriate here. So look for supportive people for your witness-gathering: those who will encourage you, yet help by holding you to the commitment you have made.

But the important thing, and the essence of the action: communicate the commitment. And then carry it out.

Which brings us to the next question: *when* is the best time to act?

Phrased this way, the implication is that there is a choice; unfortunately that is not always so. Sometimes the problem, and the required time for decision, is imposed by external events. You may face an arbitrary deadline, as in an election, or there may be actions by others that dictate the parameters. Driving on a highway, for example, requires defensive maneuvering and sometimes immediate action—or reaction. Being fired from a job and not having any savings to carry you for a while may do this; the decision of the other party in a relationship to now end it can also toll the curfew. Sometimes you can extend the deadline, and oftentimes you can extract a little more time to breathe in those situations that are forced upon you. However, when the circumstances are such that you do not have real flexibility of choice, you can curse your luck while doing what you have to.

But be sure that the deadline is a real one, or the time frame you have had thrust upon you is actually necessary; frequently there may be alternatives to merely accepting the apparent. For example, take the situation I just mentioned, where a man I know lost his job; he was short of funds and had a fixed and considerable monthly expense. He therefore feared he would have to take the very first job offered to him in order to pay the rent. However, several of his friends didn't want to see him do this and lent him enough money so that he could maintain a certain independence in his search. His friends' loan paid off handsomely because he was able to hold out for a job—and a salary—that more than compensated for the time he was unemployed.

But when the deadline or the demand for definite action is real, you must perform accordingly. What you should do here is delay the decision, and the deed, until the very last moment you can. I suggest this because some of the circumstances may change or others may surface, or you may acquire additional information in the interval. Or you may reevaluate your own needs, or desires, or preferences; numerous factors are involved which may become clearer if you can hold off the action for just a bit. Simply wait until you *must* act, before you do. But be careful that you don't miss the deadline by being distracted by some other matter when you should be acting on this question; give yourself enough safety time to prevent this from happening.

The question of when to act becomes important when it comes solely under your control; to know the optimum time to do so can be invaluable. And by "optimum" I mean that moment at which you have the best possible chance to succeed. You should not find this too difficult to determine if the decision involves only yourself; in this event you can pick the time at which you can deal with the matter most effectively. You can determine your own energy level, and patience level, and ability to concentrate on the action; the control is totally within you.

For example, I remember well when I decided to give up smoking. It was on a Thursday morning, and over breakfast I was reading in the *New York Times* the first Framingham report on the dangers of cigarettes. At the time I was operating a summer theater, and the season was ending that Saturday night. I realized that the pressures of my business for those next three days were too intense for me to be able to do anything as drastic as stopping the habit, which was then up to three packs a day. Therefore I chose Sunday morning as *the* day, and that's when I acted—successfully—on Thursday's decision. But had I tried to stop earlier, even moderate discouragement might have killed the decision then. Certainly it would have been a damn sight harder.

Similarly, you know your own abilities, and capabilities, and strength of will better than anyone. When you have to act on a decision, choose the time to do so on the basis of this knowledge of yourself so that you have the best possible chance of success.

Sometimes the decision is one on which you want to act as soon as possible, for your own peace of mind, so this goal becomes a determining factor. Here it becomes a matter of initiating the action as soon as is feasible, based on the care with which you have gone through all the previous steps. Usually there is no one else to be consulted; you are acting on your own, and as soon as you are ready. For example, a woman I know had been very career-oriented before she married; she gave this up for the rewards of a family. However, as she approached the age of forty she realized that her children were just about old enough to not only take care of themselves, but would probably be leaving the nest very shortly. And for her this birthday was a psychological milestone; she strongly felt that she had to get a job and renew her own life before then or she would feel washed-up and out of it. So she set that as the time frame within which to act on her decision to go back to work. This self-imposed deadline prompted her to make strong—and successful—efforts in this direction, and she is now very happy in her renaissance. Longfellow said, "Do not delay: the golden moments fly"; this woman had obviously heard the call.

Similarly, another woman I know had been struggling to keep alive a badly foundering marriage. Although she was smart enough to see that it would probably go under, she kept hoping that it would improve and therefore kept avoiding the decision that had to be faced. One day, however, she realized that her daughter, who was just a year old, was rapidly getting old enough to soon be dramatically affected by a parental split; she recognized that the decision had to be made then and, if it *was* to split, *then* was also *when*. She immediately and carefully analyzed the whole situation and decided that there was no realistic chance for the marriage; she made the hard determination and promptly got a divorce.

Sometimes you have to set your own deadline as to when you must decide, and act. Circumstances in the situation, which you now are fully aware of because of all the gathering of information you have done, set the time frame. For example, a Broadway producer I know had a play in rehearsal, and he was aware that it was in trouble. He believed that the underlying problem was probably the director, but he wasn't absolutely certain. To bring in a replacement, whom he already had in mind, and to give this man sufficient time to try to fix the production (yet without delaying the opening, for which there was no money), required a certain minimum number of hours of work. And so, knowing how much time was required for this major repair, the producer simply counted back and knew that he had until that cutoff moment to make, and to act on, the possible decision to replace the director. This was his effective deadline. Before then, he could make the change; doing so later would be suicidal.

Then there are the decisions and their actions that involve the participation or reaction of others. You may initiate the matter, and you may therefore be able to control the timing of when the action is taken or begun on the decision you have made. But if you also want someone to react favorably to your problem, you have to consider the situation from his point of view. Of particular concern is his receptiveness: what are his physical and emotional states when you present the matter for his reaction? What is his attitude likely to be?

In effect, you must try to determine the best time to sell your decision; that is, when will the other person be most willing to accept your choice, or go along with what you want? What is this person's mood, and what are the relevant circumstances? It would be sheer stupidity to ask someone for a job on a Friday afternoon, for example. And Monday morning, when the desk with the previous week's unfinished business is returned to, is almost as bad—unless you can clearly demonstrate your ability to help clear it off. There is a proper time for everything, and it usually requires only a little common sense to determine what that optimum moment may be. So before doing anything, just stop and think logically: if you were he, when would the best time be for someone to approach you with the action you are about to hit him with?

Sometimes you can establish a deadline for the other person, so that you will benefit by not wasting your time. For example, my dentist has this admonition on his appointment card, which is given or sent to each patient to confirm the date: "There will be no charge for broken appointments if this office is notified 24 hours in advance." Isn't that a nice way to be told you had better not cancel too late for him to use the time? And that he will charge you if you do?

There are other ways to set deadlines, too. Sometimes, when I go into a meeting at which there will be several would-be actors who love to talk, thereby wasting everyone's time as well as delaying the solution of the matter, I announce at the beginning of the meeting that I have to leave at a certain hour, whether or not the deal is concluded. Usually when my time is up, it is. Or, when I have a client who has trouble making up his mind, I help him do it by setting *his* deadline. I send him a copy of a letter I have written to our adversary, along with a note saying that I believe this is the way to handle the matter and, unless I hear to the contrary from him by a stipulated day, I shall assume his approval and send the letter as drafted. Generally, I get a simple acceptance of my proposal. And even if I don't get a response, I am still free to act.

There is another *when* that is within your control, yet requires the action of others once you have precipitated it: you must know when to pass the buck. That is, you must know when to delegate to others the action, and sometimes the initial authority, to decide whether or not to even take the action. You have to recognize that other people are capable of making decisions and carrying them out, and that some of the pressure can be taken off you by others to whom you can assign this responsibility. Some people I know waste a good deal of their time that could be more profitably spent because they are unable or unwilling to allow a relatively minute decision to be made by another. If you suspect you may be one of these compulsive doers, you would profit from re-reading the section on priorities. I would even suggest you do it now.

Timing really comes down to a very simple point: what makes the best sense? For when you put all the facts together and think about the problem and the people involved and what you want to accomplish, the logic of the situation will virtually dictate the optimum *when*. You will find it very difficult now, with all you have done up to this point, to pick the wrong time. If you're in doubt as to when to act, just ask yourself the standard question of what makes the best sense, and you're sure to come up with the most intelligent, and the best, time to do it.

Of course, it is always possible that even with the careful use of your logic, you still are not sure of this optimum moment. If this is the case then you should just fall back on the old standby, the right brain. For more often than not your instinct has been telling you what to do and when to do it; again, you simply have to trust yourself and your intuition. You do this already in all those instantaneous, reflexive decisions you make: physical activities (driving, again, is a prime example), as well as immediate questions that require what we call "snap judgment" are this kind of action. Even impulsive behavior spontaneously arising from a legitimate feeling is acceptable. These are all right-brain actions, made on the spur of the moment, and fully to be depended on.

But beware always those dangerous fantasies based on wishful thinking, and the unfounded hopes that go hand in hand with them; these are not the product of the right brain. You know when its intelligence is at work. You and I have too often made the call, or taken the action that we really knew intuitively was ill-timed, yet we acted on impetuousness and rashly overruled the instinct and the perception that is our right-brain intelligence.

Unfortunately, impatience and its corollary, rashness, are two of the biggest dangers in choosing the optimum time to act, and you must be very careful to always curb them and keep them in check lest they destroy you. You cannot act with undue haste or out of the dictates of emotion; such behavior is not right-brain but is in spite of it. Almost always impatience or rashness results in an act that is later regretted. Try to avoid any impulsiveness in your behavior; we have all been in the situation of agreeing too fast to do something and then, immediately afterward, wondering why we allowed ourselves to get trapped into compliance. Such actions are usually based on our emotional insecurities, or our programming, or both, and we can best avoid these situations if we learn to say, "Let me think about it," rather than, "Yes, I'll do it." Then, take a moment to think (left brain) about the action; you may then still decide to go ahead with it but now you will have the reassurance that you did not do so impetuously.

And be careful of the rashness that comes out of emotion, especially temper and its tantrums. For example, a woman I know got into a silly argument with her employer. Although the dispute had no real importance to either of them, it quickly—and unforgivably—escalated into one out of all proportion to the initial cause, with the woman angrily quitting her job and slamming out of the office in indignation and hurt. And all the while she was participating in this nonsensical melodrama, she knew not only that she was going to quit, but also that it was very stupid of her to do so. Yet she allowed it to happen.

In this situation, once the drama began there was no choice of *when;* everything just seemed to get out of hand because of the uncontrolled emotions. And my point is that you cannot allow this to happen; you must always be aware of when *not* to do something, just as much as you try to determine the best time *to* do it. Some people count to ten and others bite their tongue to stop the momentum of anger. Do either or both; just don't let yourself become carried away by rash overreaction. In a sense this is akin to determining the other person's receptiveness; don't try to push a budding relationship into marriage too soon. Similarly, being anxious to make a business deal should not also make you impatient; I have made a great deal of money for clients and myself by being just a little aloof. Playing hard to get is not as much a manipulative game as it is good strategy, whether left or right brain. Keep this in mind when you must decide on when to make the call, or do the act.

The other side of this coin is procrastination; it is as big a danger as impatience in determining the optimum *when.* Delaying the moment of action may minimize the anxiety of making a decision, at least superficially, but such avoidance does not remove the problem. And so the basic, underlying tension not only remains but often becomes unduly aggravated. Shakespeare said, "Delays have dangerous ends," and I agree. Once you have made your decision, you should act on it as soon as it is feasible and proper. To delay the action for reasons that are not appropriate or pertinent to the actual need is to court disaster—or, at least, a continuation of the underlying problem and its consequent unhappiness.

For example, the idea of giving a dead marriage "another three months" to be "sure" is nonsense. You know by this stage of your decision that nothing about the relationship is going to change, especially the other person. Or if you are being exploited in a relationship and you remain in it, then it is your responsibility— and your fault—as much as it is that of the other person. To stay and continue to take the punishment is not very healthy; know when to run! And the answer to that *when*, provided you have carefully taken all the steps leading up to this decision and this act, is *now*.

So beware of the false hopes, and the rationalizations, and the basic lack of self-respect; examine very carefully what is happening in your head if you find that you are delaying the act once you have made the decision to do it. Take courage, and take strength: do what must be done *now*.

Sometimes there *are* extenuating circumstances, and of course these must be taken into account. A woman I know realized that she had to end a relationship she was in, for it did not give her enough fulfillment. However, the man she was living with had just graduated from law school and was studying for his bar exams, which were to be given several months later. Since she did not want to feel any guilt at placing additional pressure on him at such a stressful time, she decided to stay until the tests were over, pretending that all was well. However, once he had taken the exams, she packed and left. The few months in this charade had not really upset her that much because she knew what she was going to do, and when. Also, she realized that her delay in acting on her decision was for a humane purpose. Her delay was not a rationalization, but a very healthy thing to do.

You must bear in mind one more consideration when you act on your decision, and this matter is probably one of the most important, and most obvious, of all that I have said throughout. It is simply this: when you have made your decision and you have acted on it, make the further commitment to give this decision a fair shot. Whatever the action may be that you have decided upon, do it wholeheartedly. Don't hold back; halfhearted actions produce halfway solutions. If you take a new job, be prepared to do everything you can to make a success of it. If you take a lover, know that you cannot ever let down on the determination and the effort to make the relationship work. Of course, you now have the added advantage of confidence: you know how well thought out your decision is, and you know how well prepared you are, no matter what its outcome. So any fear you might have had should be alleviated, and the commitment therefore should be easier to make. Just be sure that whatever your action, you make it fully, and completely, and positively.

You owe it to yourself to do so.

15

Appraising the Results
of Your Decisions

In a recent survey conducted by a popular magazine in order to determine what contributes to happiness, the question was asked, "How happy are you?" A number of the respondents requested their score on the questionnaire, and asked to be told if it was high enough for them to consider themselves happy.

Ludicrous, isn't it: judge us, please, and tell us how we feel? The sad thing about this is that these people have no sense of introspection and self-knowledge. They seem to be utterly incapable of appraising themselves and making up their minds about their own state of mind.

But I believe that at this stage of the game you must make exactly such an appraisal of yourself. You must sit back and examine, carefully and objectively and, above all, honestly, the decisions you have made, so that you can do two things: you should see if they can be improved, and you should learn from them so that you can make even better choices in the future. This appraisal is the last step in the decision-making process and, like the others, it should be done automatically, at least for those decisions that are worth the time.

Now, whether or not a decision is successful is as personal and subjective a determination as the question of whether a person is happy, so only you can evaluate the relative merits of the outcome. And by now you are surely aware that making a good decision does not guarantee a good outcome. You may have made the best decision possible under the circumstances, and it still may turn out wrong. This does not mean that your decision-making process is at fault. It simply means that in almost all situations where decisions are required you obviously do not have control over the ultimate results, and thus they do not always turn out exactly the way you would like them to. Therefore, in evaluating the outcome, you should not be defensive nor feel self-critical; you should simply be as honest and objective about the result as you can.

And this should be so even if you have to admit that you may have made a bad decision; unfortunately, we all do from time to time. You should attempt to understand as much as you can about the outcome, so that if it is not what you expected or wished it to be, you still may be able to bring about some improvement. Or, at least, you may learn enough so that you can prevent the same thing from happening again when you next face a similar situation. After all, this understanding is for your benefit and no one else's, and every bit of help you can get so that your decisions become better and easier to make is to be welcomed.

The primary question to ask yourself at this moment is: can this decision be improved in any way? And this should be asked whether you believe the outcome to be good, bad, or indifferent. If you think your decision has been successful, that's great, and how can you make it even better? Or if the outcome has not been too satisfactory, should you make some kind of change? How can you cut your losses? What about your insurance—the fall-back option?

Would that be better? Or have new alternatives, which may be more viable, become available? You must use hindsight as a tool, and from its vantage point see if whatever has been done can be made still better.

Fundamental to any self-appraisal is honesty. You should realize that any illusions, or delusions, or rationalizations you allow yourself at this point are purely counter-productive and even self-destructive, and you must be super-cautious that you don't allow any of this to happen to you. You must judge fairly and accurately, being aware at all times that it is your life that is at stake.

Let's first take the situation in which you believe the decision to be a good one and that, on balance, you are satisfied with its outcome. That's great, but if the matter is important enough to you, don't stop there; you should try to make it even better. See if there is anything you can do to really take advantage of its success. Look for the reactions of others; sometimes you can capitalize on them. Possibly you can build on this decision in some fashion, modifying or elaborating on it in such a way that it is further improved. For example, remember the woman who decided to limit her clothes buying to blue and green? She did this very happily for two years and then used her vast accumulation as the foundation for two new colors: brown and yellow. Again, she had no blending problems; virtually anything she bought offered innumerable permutations and combinations, thereby increasing both her enjoyment from shopping and her ease in doing so.

Also, when the initial decision is a good one, you often have to re-affirm and even intensify the commitment. Allowing the situation merely to coast along on its initial input will all too frequently mean that it's going downhill; you have to be sure that you do not allow this to happen. Accepting a job is only the beginning of the story; so is the marriage ceremony (or the moving in with the other). Such decisions require lots of tender, loving care and nurturing, and you cannot ever let down your effort. Keep working at whatever the commitment may be. Keep thinking that you're still trying to get the job or the man. And keep doing those things that will make the situation into an even better one than it is.

This, of course, is part of the continuing cost of having made the decision, and is something that you should have been aware of before making it; therefore what I am saying now is really not so new. Also, if you should waver, think back to the price you paid at the time of making and acting on the decision: do you want to lose all of this? For example, I asked a friend of mine who had stopped smoking if she ever felt like going back to the weed; she replied that she did, from time to time, but she never again wanted to go through the anguish of stopping, and so she would never again begin. The price had been high enough for the commitment to remain intact.

Let's look now at the situation where the outcome is obviously not a good one, and it is here that your self-confidence and courage will really show. It requires a strong person to be able to say, "I was wrong," but that's exactly what is now required. You have to be willing and able to admit that you made a bad decision (or at least that it turned out badly), and go on from there. And the test of a good or bad outcome is very simple. I use a variant of the Hemingway line I mentioned earlier ("What's moral is what you feel good after"). I say, "It's a good decision if I'm happy because of it, and it's a bad decision if I'm not." Very simple, and really what decision making is all about. Try it and see.

So, if the outcome is bad, you have to be smart enough to cut your losses and run. The Duke of Wellington (of Waterloo fame) was asked what he thought to be the best test of a general, to which he replied that it was "to know when to retreat, and how to do it." The person who remains in a bad situation, or allows himself to be continually exploited and even participates in it, has no one to blame but himself for taking the punishment. Fortunately, however, if you've been doing your homework, you're well prepared for this eventuality. There is the insurance, the fall-back position, that you now have ready for this retreat. You know what to do, and how to do it, and so you are not floundering at this moment. You need not panic; you need not run scared; you need not remain in the mess. You can quietly and calmly go on to this next alternative; you can figuratively add your name to the history books as a great general.

In terms of the timing of this strategy of retreat, however, you should keep a few points in mind. On the one hand, you must recognize that a certain insecurity is involved with any decision you make. You can, at this moment, see the results—or some of them—of the choice you made, but you probably haven't more than a clue as to how the other alternatives really would have turned out, had they been chosen. And so the nagging fear that one of them might have been better is always deeply unnerving. You entertain the thought that your judgment has deserted you and that you have made the worst of all possible mistakes, and you begin to feel all kinds of depression and regret. And you always feel worst when the decision was to give up something, like a relationship; even if you're sure you're right it's always like death to do.

But be aware of this unease and insecurity; recognize that they are natural and to be expected. Just don't panic because of them and retreat too soon. Be sure that your decision is a bad one before you go that route. Give it enough time. After all, you did think your choice out very carefully, and you must give a certain credence and support to your beliefs. Perhaps all you need do is make yet another attempt to achieve your goal; remember the enforced persistence of the woman who finally passed her driving test? So don't give up too soon; give your commitment a fair shot.

On the other hand, don't allow rationalizations or false pride to carry you forward when you know that the decision is wrong, and should be ended. This kind of momentum can be extremely dangerous, for it compounds the original error. Try to be as careful as you can not to allow it to happen to you. A tragic example of just such a failure to recognize danger signals is the case of the ill-fated Teton Dam, which collapsed in 1976, causing eleven deaths and property losses estimated at over a billion dollars. A House Government Operations subcommittee report on this disaster sharply criticized the Bureau of Reclamation's "compulsion to continue to build despite danger signals and warnings . . . the Teton Dam is a prime example of fulfilling the momentum to build at any cost." So be aware of the problems that may result from your decision, should they be present; don't allow yourself to get swamped in the tidal wave. Get out of there fast, and as soon as it is clear that you must.

All this has to do with the first function of your appraisal: how you can improve the decisions you have already made. Now I'd like to talk about its other, equally important aspect: how you can learn from them so that you can make even better decisions in the future. And this part of the discussion has validity as long as the decisions that we're talking about are those that you decided to make, and then acted upon, and are not decisions that went off on a tangent because of some totally unrelated event that was in no way connected with the decision itself but nonetheless had an effect on it. Obviously, if something happened which directly and substantially affected your decision as you were carrying it out, so that it was not the same thing that you actually decided to do, then it should not be your decision-making process that is under scrutiny here. Let me be very clear: I am talking about something happening over which you had no control and which you *had no reason to foresee*, but which materially affected the act itself as it was being carried out. Think, for example, of all the myriad decisions that were affected in one way or another by the recent blackout of electrical power in New York City for almost a day; these clearly cannot be considered here.

However, what you must look at, and accept responsibility for, are all those decisions that you did effectuate, and whether they were good or bad in their outcome, although I do believe that you can learn more from critically questioning the bad ones than from proudly acclaiming the good ones. But you should examine all of them to see how you can improve your decision-making process in the future; no reason why you too shouldn't be an expert in this field.

Make your examination quickly, almost instinctively if you wish; obviously we can't afford nor wish to spend a lot of time rehashing the past. But do think about each of the steps involved. Did you properly know your goals, define your problem, and collect and evaluate your information? Did you deliberate carefully and well? Did you accurately predict the cost, the risk, and the probability of success; or were you unrealistic in any of these areas? And if so, why? Were you properly prepared for any contingencies that could conceivably—and possibly did—affect the outcome? Or did you fall into any of the vast number of problems we talked about—those of self-respect, or improper thinking? Did you waste time, or confuse your priorities? Have you repeated past mistakes; or are you blindly following custom or accepting without question old, established ways? Sometimes it is easy to do this, because a pattern has been ingrained and is comfortable, albeit wrong. This can especially happen when you rationalize that what you have done in the past was right, and that "somehow" it didn't turn out the way you wanted it to.

If the decision was an out-and-out bad one, the questions might be even more pertinent, and insistent, and demanding. You should question your basic needs for doing this particular act in the first place. Were these needs healthy or neurotic? What impelled you to do this, and what triggered it? What warning signals or danger flags did you ignore, especially those of the right brain, and why did you refuse to see them? And did you make the commitment fully? Did you give it a fair shot?

These questions are particularly apropos in the case of a bad relationship—and should that be the area you are examining, you should always ask: was it ever a relationship from the beginning? Often, that's the root of the problem.

You must ask yourself all these questions and any others that may help give you some insights into the matter you are considering, and you should do your utmost to come up with honest answers. By going back over your past decisions and appraising them this way, you may be able to find some common denominators: factors that seem to continually crop up in your decisions, either good or bad. You can then use this information to help you make better decisions in the future. If the recurring factors are debilitating ones, you should go back to the pertinent material in this book and spend some extra time on it. And, should these repetitive elements be positive, capitalize on them in the future.

You must examine a very important point here, especially when you feel a decision has not been a good one. Have you, by any chance, had a change of goals that you may not have been aware of? Or, as a corollary, were there certain goals, or aspects of them, that you overlooked? Either way, the simple nonfulfillment of what these needs may be will be sufficient to ruin an otherwise well-thought-out decision, and this is therefore a question you must examine carefully. Or, sometimes, once a goal has been achieved it sometimes no longer seems that important. The investment banker I mentioned earlier feels exactly this way, and after the end of each affair she sits down with her balance sheet and amends and corrects it accordingly. And the interesting thing about this list, she recently told me, is that it is becoming increasingly right-brain oriented: she is adding more subjective and emotional qualities to it, and taking off a number of the more precisely structured and establishment-oriented details. For example, the personal attention she receives from a man has become more important to her than his behavior at dinner parties, which was previously one of her big considerations.

Probably the most important concept to bear in mind, however, as you go through this appraisal process, is that nothing is forever. Today's answers, good as they may be, only lead to tomorrow's problems; you can be certain that there will always be more decisions to face and to make. There are no finalities. Values change and create new problems; people change and do the same. So in this sense each decision is a re-birth, creating its own problems. It is a circular process; therefore you must always, and continually, examine your life with the calm realization that there is always something happening in it and to it that must then be resolved.

Which you are now beautifully equipped to do.

16

What It All Means to You

As I was laboring over this book and it began to take more and more of my time, I was continually teased about my ever finishing it. A friend spoke to me about this one day, and she referred to several of these chapters she was familiar with. "You're not taking your own advice," she said. "You have a problem and you're not facing up to it."

"What are you talking about?" I asked.

"It's simple," she replied; "you really don't want to ever end it, and so you don't know how to."

And she was right. It is time to part.

It would be nice, before we do, if I could summarize this book for you and say, "Here are the ten basic rules to remember." Unfortunately, it just won't work that way. There is a lot that goes into making a decision, as you've seen, and every bit of it is of consequence and meaning. Everything I've discussed has its place and its value; and if you are going to make better decisions in your life, you can't overlook any of it. You must constantly use it all, in its entirety, as a living, cohesive whole. As I pointed out at the beginning, this attempt on my part to break down into steps the art of making decisions is a purely arbitrary matter; there really are no lines of demarcation called chapters into which the brain sorts its product. Everything I have said about analyzing one step, for example, is as easily applied to all others. What I hope to have accomplished is that you will take some of the suggestions and ideas I have presented and put them together with your own thinking so that you come up with a meaningful and homogeneous concept of how they relate in your life, and for you. It's like a relationship: one can only offer it, not force it. Similarly, I can only say, "Here is the information. Do with it as you will."

And now you've got the knowledge. The importance of the decisions you treat with it, and how you do so, is now up to you.

You will find that, as you use this material, it will become a part of you, and your decisions will inevitably be more successful because of it. Probably you have already found this to be so. Further, this success, as I have said before, is self-breeding; the continuing and increasing confidence you gain from making successful decisions will make it easier for you to make more of them.

I hope, too, that you have come to understand and appreciate the marvel of our intelligence as I do. I have tried very hard to convey to you how deeply I respect the brain and the fascinating way it functions; I am in absolute awe of it. It is what makes us such individuals, yet still allows us to communicate so closely each with the other. The brain is also the wellspring of all our feelings of self, and of self-respect. It is what will save us from whatever morass, or Wonderland, we may be in. Unlike Alice, with its use we *do* know where we want to go.

And, knowing this, we can make the necessary commitment to ourselves: we can say, with conviction and with dignity, "This is what I am worth, and this is what I want. And I will have it."

For it all comes down to one thing; I guess if you want the

essence of this book capsulized you can put it very simply this way: you must respect yourself. You have the intelligence to deal with the world, and beyond. Therefore you must trust yourself. You must believe in yourself. And you must make your decisions accordingly. If you do, you've got it made.

Doesn't it make sense?

Index